New Worlds, New Geographies

Space, Place, and Society
John Rennie Short, *Series Editor*

New Worlds | New Geographies

John Rennie Short

Syracuse University Press

First Edition 1998
98 99 00 01 02 03   6 5 4 3 2 1

The paper used in this publication meets the minimum requirements of American National
Standard for Information Sciences—Permanence of Paper for Printed Library Materials,
ANSI Z39.48-1984. ∞™

Library of Congress Cataloging-in-Publication Data
Short, John R.
   New worlds, new geographies / John Rennie Short. — 1st ed.
     p. cm. — (Space, place, and society)
   Includes bibliographical references.
   ISBN 0-8156-0527-7 (cloth : alk. paper).
    1. Geography. I. Title. II. Series.
   G116.S55   1998
   910—dc21   97-29244

Manufactured in the United States of America

For Agnes Short (née Rennie),
     1930–1956

I dedicated this book to my mother. She died when I was four years of age. Her absence left a gaping wound in my life, a hurt that was deep but unacknowledged. When my name first began to appear in print, I could not use my full name, John Rennie Short, because the middle part was her name. I hid it: John Short. Then disguised it: John R. Short. Only in my late thirties could I use my full name because only then could I admit to myself how much I missed her. I could accept what was there by acknowledging what was absent.

   I miss her very much. I think of her often. When I was very young I wanted to write something so great that it would make her come back to life. Now that I am older, I know this is not possible. To dedicate this book to her is admitting that she is never coming back. Ever. But a harsh reality has not replaced a child's dream. There is still a miracle at the heart of our enduring relationship. This book is neither a call to life nor a final good-bye. It is more of a loving wave until we meet again.

Let sea-discoverers to new worlds have gone,
Let Maps to other, worlds on worlds have showne,
Let us possesse one world, each hath one, and is one.

—John Donne
The Good Morrow (ca. 1593)

John Rennie Short is professor of geography at the Maxwell School of Citizenship and Public Affairs, Syracuse University. He is the author of many books including *The Urban Order*, *Imagined Country: Society, Culture and Environment* and *The Humane City* and the editor of *Human Settlement*.

Contents

Introduction

An Encounter

A gaze.

A long, hard gaze.

A gaze that held us both in its grip of mutual interest and shared curiosity.

His face was old. Sculpted by the passing of time, the experience of pain and regret. But it was the face of a survivor. My face. Always hidden from me. Only available to me in the distortion of a mirror. What did he see in my face? What stories did it tell? He did not say.

We were separated by the thickness of glass. He was inside a white, transit van smeared with the deep-red dust of the Australian interior. I was walking across the manicured lawn to the library. The van stopped at an intersection. I looked at the van. Inside, a dozen old men sat impassive but erect. They were strange. Old, black heads, thin shoulders. That's all I could see. They looked exotic, out of place in the all-white campus, a reminder of a distant country, an echo of another time. The man, one of the dozen occupants, looked at me. I looked at him.

We were separated by more than the glass, connected by more than the look. The space between us was a space of separation, as well as connection, a zone of indifference as well as the setting for an encounter. Many things joined us, many things kept us apart.

The gaze lived with me for some time. It still does. I can see the impassive face looking at me. And me looking at him.

I didn't know what it all meant. I still don't. The event touched me someplace deeper than my intellect. The encounter has resonated in my imagination down the years. It has stayed with me, a source of reinterpretation, an occasion for thought and imaginings. I wanted to understand my silent, seeing partner. I wanted to understand myself. I wanted to understand the gaze.

Many things joined us. Many things kept us apart. In that chance encounter, I believed, there was something of greater significance than a chance meeting of an old black man and a young white man, an Australian and a European. As the image of the gaze burned bright in my memory through the years it took on the status of a force field for my ideas, a kind of magnetic force field in which my ideas, like iron filings, were given direction, orientation, spacing, and shape.

Events take place. The significance of any event is in its spacing in time, its timing in space. Canberra. Autumn 1985. Underneath a deep-blue, cloudless sky. In the grounds of the Australian National University. We were both visitors to that beautiful, planned city. I at the beginning of a two-year visit. A visiting academic. Escaping from what? Arriving to what? He, and this only became known to me later, was a tribal elder, part of an Aboriginal demonstration to lobby the government about land rights. My interest in space and place was academic, his more personal, more immediate.

Our different perspectives was one of the things that separated me from him. I, like him, was both a guardian and a prisoner of a certain way of seeing things. We could stand on the same spot yet see vastly different worlds. The horizon of my sight was not the limit of his vision. And there was something else. There was an attitude. When I looked at him, my seeing was not an innocent seeing, my seeing was refracted through values, beliefs, histories, and geographies. In that seeing was condensed the contact between the modern and the ancient.

We are members of societies that are changing, that have their own trajectory through historical space. We are all members of communities that are as much in the process of becoming as being. I was coming from a modern world turning into postmodern, and he was coming from an ancient world being quickly transformed into postancient. Were postmodern and postancient the same thing? Were we meeting at the same point in time, starting from different directions but ending up in the same location? Was the gaze an act of historical communion linking past with present? Then with now? Me with him?

Another Encounter

I met him in August 1991.

It was at a political geography conference in Prague. He led a field trip to the coal-mining area of Bohemia, north of Prague. He sat at the front of the bus, microphone in hand, speaking in English, pointing out sites of interest, telling us about the landscape unfolding outside the large windows. On the few occasions when I have been in the same position I found it an unnerving experience. You speak into a metal object that amplifies your voice to unnatural proportions, and your audience is behind you. To give a lecture to an unseen audience, talking to a crowd behind your back, is a difficult thing to do well. He was speaking, for him, in a foreign language. A metal object, an unseen audience, and a foreign language. Impressive. And he seemed interested, not just going through the motions. Even more impressive.

Not far out of the city of Prague, he pointed out a large imposing building. It was a prison. He mentioned that he had spent a brief time there as a prisoner. He didn't make a big deal out of it. The comment was made in passing, to give some color, a more personal touch to the description. The day was depressing. Passing through a coal-mining landscape is never heartening; but the air was so foul, so heavy with pollution that it lay on my chest like a lead weight. I did not get a chance to speak to him. But the next day I found myself next to him outside the conference room at the university.

"So what were you in prison for?" I asked.

"Attending a demonstration," he replied in perfect English. "An antigovernment demonstration. I was picked up. But I only spent one night in jail." I had the image of the old society, like a chronic drunk trying to keep balance, unstable, ready to fall at any moment. I knew the change had been quick. No more than two weeks in November 1989 from the first mass demonstrations to the overthrow of the regime.

"It must have been exciting?" I asked him. "Knowing that it was going to fall."

"I didn't know that," he replied. "Even the day before the fall, I still thought we would have to wait five, maybe even ten years before we could change the system." I found that incredible. Here was a dissident, someone who was always looking for the cracks, the weaknesses, the fracture lines that the official state tried to conceal and patch up with consensus. Even someone with this critical gaze still thought, on the very eve of the huge rupture, that the system would last for years, maybe even a decade.

He was young. Mid-twenties, maybe even late twenties. Here was a genuine dissident. Not one of those who emerged late from out of the woodwork of the old regime with the too-insistent cry that they were always anti-Communist, nor one of those who had done well out of the old system and determined to do equally well out of the new society. No, this was genuine critic, a concerned citizen who attended a demonstration when the old regime still seemed secure. There was no way of knowing for sure, but just something about him gave me the feeling that his commitment to social change and improvement would continue into the emerging Czech society.

I continue to remember the meeting and our discussion. Three observations. First, the young man was a creator of a new world, not one of your political leaders who is remembered in the history books or whose photograph is always in the newspaper. But, along with all the other anonymous people, he helped to bring about a change that two generations of political leaders had been unable, and to a certain extent unwilling, to disturb. In his youth he was still uncompromised by convention. The world weariness that breeds a tired cynicism and a passive acceptance of the status quo, which often overtakes people in their middle years, was still too far ahead of him to constitute a threat to his optimism. His enthusiasm and commitment were like a bright light that made my pessimism and cynicism all the darker and narrower.

Second, I felt envious. He was on the right side. Not only the good side but the side that won. Integrity and success. What a wonderful combination for a political activist. When I had been on the right side they had not won. And when I had won, I was not sure I was on the right side. Maybe it was age. Perhaps I was jealous of his youth, of his untarnished innocence, of his part in a great transformation. I still am.

Third, the meeting filled me with hope. Part of me wanted to write off his enthusiasm as a function of his age, something that would be knocked out of him as he got older. Maybe I wanted him to be more like me. Something still does. But another part of me could look into his face and see a new world. Not a naïve vision of a world where the lion will lie down with the lamb, but a world still emerging, subject to all sorts of constraints but, for the first time in over fifty years, a world where freedom was on the agenda, emancipation was a reality, and hope an acceptable currency. For how long I am not sure. As I get older, I sometimes see the good times in our lives as only temporary clearings in a dark forest where demons come out unbidden and unrequested. But meeting this young man reconfirmed my optimism, my sense of hope. The city of our meeting enhanced the feeling. Prague. Two years earlier a regime had collapsed, had been forced to collapse by the weight of public pressure. Enough people had said no to undermine the legitimacy of a state. A state with armed soldiers, extensive surveillance, police, strong powers of threat and coercion. Even a state with all this power at its disposal could not withstand the weight of popular protest and resistance.

The big changes in the world refer to more than what happened in Prague or the fall of communism in Eastern Europe. There is a sense of fundamental change in the world. Words like *post-Fordist, postmodern, new world order* all give some indication of a radical rupture between the past and the present. That was then, this is now. We know what the then was. We are not so sure of the now. And we are only dimly aware of what the future will look like. We have lost that most comforting illusion: the present is a continuation of the past. More than ever before, L. P. Hartley's phrase has a truer ring: the past is a foreign country where they do things differently. The fall of communism was not a cause of the change; it was an indication of the scale, depth, and magnitude of the change sweeping the world.

This book is not a textbook. Neither is it a research monograph. It is a set of essays as much personal as analytical, more big picture than detailed analysis and broader rather than deeper. Some of the chapters had a previous life in journals and books. Their precise provenance is given in the Publishing Acknowledgments. They draw upon just some of my research and writing over the past five years. I have rewritten these and added new ones. Taken together, they represent my attempt to understand a long gaze with an Aborigine and my response to the envy, encouragement, and hope I felt when I spoke to a young Czech geographer. The book articulates my attempt to make sense of a changing world.

This is a personal book: perhaps fitting in an era when we are shifting from metanarratives to personal stories. It is written at a particular time in my life, a time of both looking backward and forward, an evaluation of the past and a contemplation of the future. It is appropriate, therefore, to give some kind of introduction to the author.

On The Periphery of the Periphery

I was born in October 1951 in the small town of Stirling in Scotland. My father, aged eighteen, was not present for my birth; this was not unusual at the time, but he was further away than most. He was in the army drafted to fight in Korea for a war he could not understand, for an ideology he did not share. A confirmed Socialist with Communist leanings, he was the wrong age at the wrong time; but lacking money or influence, he became one more foot soldier in the imperial collision between East and West. Thus from the very moment of my birth through all of my youth and early adulthood, my life took place against the background of the great divide between East and West.

I was in the West geographically but not emotionally. Being born into a working-class family in Scotland meant that the ideology of Western supremacy, tinged with British imperialism, could not take hold, condensing as it did notions of English nationalism and anticommunism, which my family never believed in nor subscribed to. Then there was my paternal grandmother. Milan Kundera once described the contemporary period as an age of forgetting. My grandmother forgot nothing. She had a folk memory. One example: she remembered the virulent anti-working-class sentiments of Winston Churchill, his war against the miners in the Great Strike; she could admire his wartime leadership but never trust him. She remembered that he was a class warrior as much as a wartime hero. My grandmother could remember things that governments soon forgot for the sake of compromise, pragmatism, and new geopolitical realities. She remembered that three young men from a local regiment were taken out into an orchard of orange trees just outside Jerusalem in 1947 and shot in the back of the head by the Irgun. Freedom fighters for the new Israel or terrorists: choose your nomenclature according to your prejudice. She passed on folk memories and stories. I remember being told that rich people wanted war because they made more money. I remember her distaste for the titled and the wealthy. I remember her love of learning. I remember her giving me spelling exercises. Book learning and political education combined in a loving way that I was never taught at school nor university. This background insulated me from the national chauvinism inherent in formal education and the political bias of the mass media.

I was raised on the periphery of the periphery. Scotland was on the edge of the English state called Britain. That was one periphery. Another was of a working-class family that did not share an optimistic belief in the capitalist order and had a commitment to the shining promise of the Soviet Union rather than the reality of state socialism. The promise of communism, rather than the reality of state socialism, was of working people having more control and power over their lives. My family knew from experience that the "free" market was not all that free for everyone. The notion of an economy managed by and for the workers was a part of our family ideology as opposed to the official ideology, transmitted by the media.

This national and social peripheralization meant my position in the great schism between East and West, which stood in the background of my life, was that of an uncomfortable straddler. I was of the West and in the West but not for the West. The East was the point of criticism for the status quo of the West. And I never quite believed all the anti-Communist news and information. I believed it was partly fueled by the desire to denigrate the great promise of communism, the formalized hopes and dreams of my family. Communism was not just the failed god of the intellectuals—it was the political backbone to a Scottish working-class culture embodying as it did concepts of equality and fairness.

Later as a student, I affected the Marxism that was then fashionable. My position became slightly more complex. The reality of the Soviet Union was sullied, but the promise was still there; a better society was still possible, capable of future emergence from a compromised present. But my growing maturity was matched by a growing realization that the bright new society would not appear in the East, that capitalism seemed the more resilient. I remember visiting Czechoslovakia in 1983. I went to play soccer, and this gave me an opportunity to see the lives of ordinary people. I was not a tourist nor on an official visit, just a member of a soccer team playing Slovak soccer teams. Wandering around the city of Bratislava and nearby towns before the games, I remember the grayness, the pollution, and the overwhelming sense of a society in cynical limbo, summed up by the giant photographs of party hacks looking down on a sullen population. I could remember a society on the verge of collapse, but that would be to remember through the prism of later events. At the time I just remember a grayness, neither the blackness of total despair nor the brightness of the brave new world, just the gray reality of a society compromised by the yawning chasm between its brilliant rhetoric yet dismal performance. But to return to Britain from Czechoslovakia in 1983 was to return from a bankrupt communism to a socially impoverished Thatcherism. If this was the choice, I wanted to say no thanks to both of them.

"This Baffling Geography"

The changes in our personal lives can sometimes mirror the broader swirls of history. In 1991 when I met the young Czech geographer, I was approaching my fortieth birthday. I was affecting my own compromises, experiencing the disappointment caused by the contrast between early dreams and my current life. A new leader in the Kremlin, a whole new world of emotions opening up within me. I experienced my own personal *glasnost*, my own emotional *perestroika* as the cold war ended, the Communist leadership crumbled and the Berlin Wall was pulled down. A process of individuation and political restructuring in some kind of strange step. A new world order. A new personal and political geography being created. Me and global geopolitics in some crazy sync.

In a book review the writer James Baldwin once wrote,

When more time stretches behind than stretches before one, some assessments, however reluctantly and incompletely, begin to be made. Between what one wishes to become and what one has become there is a momentous gap, which will now never be closed. And this gap seems to operate as one's final margin, one's last opportunity, for creation. And between the self as it is and the self as one sees it, there is also a distance, even harder to gauge. Some of us are compelled, around the middle of our lives, to make a study of this baffling geography, less in the hope of conquering these distances than in the determination that the distance shall not become any greater (Baldwin 1967).

The search for some sort of meaning and understanding is, at root, deeply personal. Think of the chapters of this book as small maps of my own, particular "baffling geography."

In this book I want to look at this new world. In part 1 I consider the notion of the new world order, its relationship to the nation-state and the urban region. In part 2 I examine alternative methods of social science research. Each part has essays that range from the general to the particular and that seek to tell stories in that difficult terrain between theory and case study. I will seek to make the connections between global changes, urban transformation, and the reappraisal of the academic enterprise. Together, the essays try to make some kind of sense out of the rupture of our world, the changes in our cities, and the need for a new angle of vision. I will seek to show the connections, obvious and not so obvious, between the new world order, urban change, and the pursuit of scholarly integrity. Part 3 takes a very different tack. The linear narrative of the first two parts is now replaced with an A to Z of postmodernity. An alternative textual strategy is employed to give a handle to the concept, practice, and ideas of postmodernity. I take postmodernity to be just one way of labeling our present predicaments, concerns, worries, and hopes. Part 3 thus continues the concern with the contemporary world.

The book considers the new world in which I now find myself. Part 1 considers the new world order, the relationship of the state to this world order, and the emerging new urban order. Part 2 is a series of reflections of the academic world where I make my living and establish much of my identity. The final part of the book is an ambitious attempt to make sense of many of the trends, postures, and debates centering around the theme and language of postmodernity. This word has become a catchall for many of the new debates and movements. To unpack the meaning of the term is to understand much about the contemporary world.

This book comes from the shifting position and fixed location of one observer whose view is both enhanced and restricted by his nationality, gender, age, race, and ethnicity. This book is the reflections of a reluctant postmodern, a resident alien, an academic geographer trying to make sense of his baffling geography.

Part One

New Worlds

1

The New World Order?

In the final decades of the second millenium, the term *new world order* was heard more often. We should treat with immense care any designation with the adjective *new* because on closer inspection the new can seem very old. *New world order* is no exception. In 1922 the American political geographer Isaiah Bowman, looking at the world reshaped by the First World War and its immediate aftermath, published a book entitled *The New World: Problems in Political Geography*. Over seventy-five years, later it still makes salutary reading. On page 2, under a section entitled "New World Problems," Bowman listed a number of questions (see table 1.1). Some of these questions look rather quaint. Nowadays, we do not use the term *native* in such a context, and some of the countries cited by Bowman would not figure on current lists of concern. But the really striking fact is the contemporary feel of his questions: the survival of fragile democracies, the concern with armaments, the precarious rights of certain minorities and the dangers involved in the commercial rivalry between nations all continue to be issues of pressing contemporary concern.

3

Reading Bowman gives some credence to the notion that history is a succession of cycles, a constant repetition of recurring motifs. But human history is more than just a reciting of old songs and retelling of familiar stories. Change does occur. Although the new of the new world order has exaggerated claims to uniqueness, it is a very different order from that of the preceding one. Bowman's new world was one in which most of the world was under the control of a few powerful colonial powers. In the intervening period, there has been the successful struggle against colonial power and the consequent growth of independent states. Motifs may recur but they do so against a constantly changing background. The context for the age-old power struggles is forever in flux.

How then are we to use the term *new world order?* With some care. At its loosest it is a mixture of hype and hope. We should be wary of the hype that is part of a consumer culture fixation with the new and look for links with the near and distant past. Comparisons with other times of convulsive political and social change, as in the aftermath of the First World War or even further back to the end of the Napoleonic Wars when a new Europe was being created, will reveal similarities in the search for order in a world whose stability has been shattered. We should also be careful, however, of naive hope entirely replacing sober analysis. Problems still persist and the dawn of a new world order may only be the view from the affluent suburbs of the rich world.

Behind the political hype and the pious hope the term does have some meaning. It cannot be easily dismissed. Its appearance and usage do refer to real and important changes in the world. In essence it refers to the decline of the old dichotomy between East and West, the decline of the Soviet Empire and the unraveling of state socialism in Eastern Europe. These are momentous changes.

Table 1.1
Problems of the New World in 1922

Whatever the faults of the old world, it was at least what a business man would call a "going concern"; can the *new* world be set going in an orderly manner?

How much of the old world is left?

What new boundaries, concessions, colonies, mandataries, spheres of influence, and protectorates now appear on the map of the world?

What kind of people compose the new states?

Will the new democracies survive,—in Poland and Jugo-slavia and Austria, for example,—or are some of the experiments in self-government likely to fail?

What elements of economic strength and weakness has each of the new states, and each of the old states whose resources have been either increased or diminished by treaty?

The large and powerful states—the "great powers"—have, from this time forward, a new set of rights and responsibilities. How will these responsibilities be met?

Will the strong states administer their colonies and protectorates in the interest of the natives?

Can the terrible burden of armaments be reduced by common agreement?

Has the day of deliverance come for the oppressed minorities of the earth, those who have hitherto been persecuted because of differences between themselves and the majority or ruling class in race, religion, or social custom?

How far can the protection of minorities be carried? Can the so-called minorities treaties stand, or do they threaten the integrity of the unwilling signatory states—Poland, Czecho-Slovakia, Rumania, Jugo-Slavia and Greece?

Will strong nations continue the struggle for trade privileges, raw materials, and economic zones, with the prospect of war between them if they cannot realize their commercial and political ambitions otherwise?

In short, will the changes in the political and economic geography of the world spell peace or war, strength or weakness, in the years immediately before us?

SOURCE: Isaiah Bowman (1922) *The New World: Problems in Political Geography*. London. Harrap. (Emphasis in original.)

Retreat from Empire

From 1945 to the late 1980s, world politics was dominated by the division of the world into two competing blocs headed by two unequal superpowers, the United States and the Soviet Union. Their respective spheres of influence mapped out the geopolitical terrain of global interaction. Powerful forces in each country had a stake in the continued antagonism. The military-industrial complex in each country saw in the threat of the "other" a ready-made excuse for continued expansion. A spiral in arms buildup occurred; the expansion in one area of a superpower's arsenal was seen by the other as a threat and was met with a buildup in arms that the other saw as further threat . . . and so it went on, a dance of destruction between two partners keeping up with a music of rising tempo.

The posture of antagonism petrified social change in each country. In the Soviet Union, critics of the regime could easily be branded as traitors working for the West. Any major reform that looked as if it might introduce market forces were stillborn by the antagonism with the market-driven enemy. While other Eastern Bloc countries had privatization schemes of varying degrees of success, the Soviet Union was still stuck in the vicelike grip of the central plan. In the United States, programs of social reform were tainted by association with socialism and communism. While all Western countries had social welfare programs the United States was stuck in the time warp of the 1950s; to be poor in the United States of America was to have the poorest medical, welfare, and educational services of any rich capitalist country. The cold war had many casualties, one of the biggest being meaningful social reform in the two superpowers.

The remark of a US president (it has been attributed to both Franklin Roosevelt and Johnson) that a South American dictator was "a sonofabitch, but he's our sonofabitch" captures the essence of the imperial role. What was important was maintaining and extending one's sphere of influence around the world at the expense of the other superpower. This was the primary objective, and it was achieved through support of "friendly" elites. The most important thing was the external orientation of these elites and not their domestic role; their "friendliness" was measured primarily in regard to their support for the superpower, not with respect to the treatment of their own people. How else can we explain the paradox that the United States, in the name of democracy and liberty, could support evil regimes, corrupt dictatorships, and ruling elites who ran states best described as clepto-cracies. One example: President Mobutu had ruled Zaire for the past thirty years, installed and propped up by the CIA because of his anti-Communist sympathies. Even conservative estimates place his personal fortune, looted from the state at $10 billion. That would buy a lot of schools and hospitals. While the country went bankrupt, Mobutu kept up an imperial lifestyle in Europe, including a suite at a Swiss luxury hotel, a ranch in Portugal, a castle in Spain, and houses in Paris, Brussels, and Venice.

In Eastern Europe the Soviet Union supported repressive Communist parties held in power only by the presence of Soviet tanks rather than by any mandate from the people. The direct intervention of the two superpowers can be explained with reference to the collapse of these collaborative elites; for the Soviets, direct intervention arose, as in Hungary in 1956, Czechoslovakia in 1968, and Afghanistan in 1979. Parallel interventions by the United States occurred in Vietnam (1959–73) and around the world, including Lebanon, Dominican Republic, Panama, Guate-mala, and a host of others. These interventions were necessitated by the crumbling power base of "friendly" elites.

The imperial posture was expensive. The costs were borne by the two superpowers in different ways. In the Soviet Union, lim-its were placed on the production of consumption goods. The country could build intercontinental missiles, but people had to form a long line to buy a car. In the United States, limits were placed on investment in human resources. Thus it had the most sophisticated military technology but infant mortality rates and literacy rates that, for a very rich country, were some of the worst in the developed world. Each superpower had to pay the price of global reach and imperial overstretch. It was an uneven struggle. The United States was richer and did not face the legitimation cri-sis endemic to the Soviet Union. The United States was rich enough to maintain an informal empire and maintain living standards high enough to keep a measure of consensus between the state and the people. Barely two out of three eligible voters have cast their vote in recent presidential elections, and the political process is dominated by those with money; and so we are not speaking of a fully articulated participatory democracy. The United States did not have the endemic conflict between governed and governing that was the order in the Soviet Union, however. The crunch came for the Soviet Union in the 1980s. Declining oil revenues, spiraling military costs, and the atrophying of the whole planned economy were the background to the popular discontent. Gorbachev's promotion to president in 1985 was, in retrospect, an indication of the depth of the crisis; his ascendancy, a mark of the perception of the problem at the very highest political levels. The inauguration of *perestroika* and *glasnost* and the bold initiatives at the international level, especially in the area of arms reductions that came with Gorbachev's leadership, all heralded major transformations. The failed coup of 1991 showed how far things had changed. The old repressive structure could no longer contain popular expression of change. And in the aftermath of the coup came the virtual dismantling of the Communist Party stranglehold on power and the fracturing of the Union into the constituent republics.

For the United States, the ending of the cold war was not so dramatic, but it was equally momentous. It no longer had the "evil other" to structure its worldview and to legitimate its imperial role. It was like a Siamese twin that had lost its partner. Part of its lifeblood came from the presence of the other. Its domestic political stances and military-economic structure were predicated on the existence of the Soviet "threat." Without its "other" the United States had to establish a new role in the changed world order. But it was a role in which military and economic dominance had become disentangled. The United States remains the single biggest military power, the only one with effective global reach; but its economic power is being undermined by a strong Japan and an emerging Europe. And its military power is as much a handicap as an asset. Too much of research and development funding has been associated for too long with military technology. Its more successful economic competitors have spent far more on developing consumer goods for a world market. The United States is like a boxer who has gone through fifteen rounds only to find that someone else on the sidelines is picking up the prize money. And also like a battered prizefighter at the end of a grueling contest, the United States is undergoing a period of introspection as it takes stock of the changed world and tries to figure out a new role.

For many domestic critics and social reformers in the United States, this is a period of renewed hope, as they feel that much needed domestic reform, continually delayed because of the imperial venture, can at last be addressed. For others, the new world order is something to fear and fret over. The end of the bipolar world, coupled with the relative economic decline of the United States, has created a social disaffection that, at its wildest margins, is represented in the militia movement and the rise of rightwing groups who see the federal government and its involvement in global institutions as a selling out of their national heritage. On a radio program, Pat Buchanan said, "when I hear the term new world order I reach for my gun." The rise of armed militias represent a uniquely US response to changing political realities and threatening economic change. During the cold war the conspiracy theorists, patriots and the state all shared the same enemy. National consensus was achieved through economic growth and a common foe. With the fall of communism, globalization, and the economic difficulties of the middle-class, consensus is no longer so apparent. Globalization, so the arguments go, creates job loss and wage cuts. The new world order is not something to celebrate but something to fear and resist. The scapegoating of the external Communists has turned into the search for internal enemies.

A similar trend can be noted in Russia. The loss of empire, economic turmoil, and the perceived loss of superpower status has fueled Russian nationalism. There are no Russian equivalents of the US militia movement, but there is a similar grassroots discontent that can find expression in xenophobic movements.

New world order is used by politicians and intellectuals as a welcome trend, an inauguration of a more peaceful, less divided, world. For many people in the United States and Russia, it is the harbinger of economic decline, loss of sovereignty, and decline of national power. In Russia the discontent is reflected in the return to power of Communists and an anti-Western rhetoric. At the extreme in the United States, it is seen as a conspiracy between the federal government and anti-US forces that has to be resisted, contested, and defeated. The bombing of the Alfred P. Murrah Federal Building in Oklahoma City on April 19, 1995, was only the most visible and hideous manifestation of this paranoia.

Enduring Tensions in the New World Order

The old bipolar structure that defined the world order is now over. The US–Soviet enmity will, like Rome and Carthage, dissolve into history. That is something to be applauded. The buildup of arms, the repression of dissent, especially behind the iron curtain, and the support of authoritarian regimes by both superpowers around the world did much to slow down, if not halt, social progress. But the new world that is emerging from the old world is not free of problems; we can identify three enduring sources of tension.

The first is the huge disparity between the rich countries of the world and the poor; the gap between the haves and the have-nots is still there and in some cases is increasing. Even in the middle-income countries that had such tremendous growth rates in the 1970s, the debt crisis is gnawing away at the very fabric of society. In countries such as Mexico and Peru, rates of malnutrition actually increased in the 1980s. The global economy is still unfair in its distribution of costs and benefits. Affluence consists of small islands in a vast ocean of poverty in the world; the poorest countries of the world have 40 percent of the world's population but less than 3 percent of the world's wealth. In this new world order, crippling poverty is still the accepted way of life, diseases are endemic, and stunted ambitions are the norm. This world is not so much postmodern as nonhuman. We can make no claim to a civilized world unless we redirect our attention to the poverty, disease, and famine that haunt the planet. There are still too many hungry people in the world. More than five thousand children die every day from the lack of clean water. That is appalling, a disgrace to human society. A truly new world order should be concerned with the eradication of poverty, malnutrition, and poor health. Even stating the goals in such a bald manner sounds utopian. But analysts can become too sophisticated. What the world order should primarily be concerned with is sustaining the dignity of all the world's citizens not just with maintaining the affluence of a minority. The concern with global fairness will be an important agenda for the next millennium.

Second, there is increasing economic competition between former political allies. From 1945 until the mid-1970s, the Western world was dominated by the United States, which was the strongest economy and the biggest military power. There was a large measure of congruence in the foreign policy of the allies. Throughout the 1970s and 1980s, the United States remained the leading military power; but, as stated earlier, its economic strength was weakened by an emerging Europe and a dynamic Japan. The economic conflict between Japan, the United States and Europe, masked throughout much of the postwar period because of continued economic growth, surfaced in the 1970s as the world economy hit recession. By the early 1990s, it became obvious that erstwhile allies were fighting an intense war of economic competition. The decline of the Soviet Union means that there is no longer a political "other" to provide the cement to bind these countries together. Conflict among them takes the form of attempts at protecting their domestic markets, fighting for overseas markets, and emerging conflict over the cost of international policing. The United States has borne the burden of military expenditure among Western powers; but with its own economic difficulties and the decline of the Soviet Empire, politicians and the electorate in the United States may well ask why the defense burden should be so unfairly distributed, especially given the economic strength of other countries such as Japan and Germany. Some indication of the changes was shown in the 1991 war for Kuwait between Iraq and an alliance of the United States and European and Arab countries. The dominant role was played by the United States, which not only sought recompense from Kuwait but also looked to a fiscal contribution from Germany and Japan commensurate with their economic power.

At the end of the twentieth century, we have seen the creation of competing trading blocs: an integrated Europe with Germany as the leading economic power, Japan with a worldwide presence but a very strong presence in Asia and the whole Pacific Rim, and an American bloc consisting of both Latin and North America with the United States as the dominant power. These three blocs will seek to protect their domestic industries and to ensure export markets. The stage is set for an era of intense international economic competition.

One of the most powerful political novels of the twentieth century was *1984*, written by the Englishman George Orwell. It was written in 1948; and although it has been seen as a commentary on totalitarian possibilities of the future, it was also an examination of contemporary trends. Forty-eight transposed is eighty-four. In the novel, the world is divided into three competing blocs: Eastasia, Eurasia, and Oceania. The tripartite division seems to have some validity when we look at the emerging economic superpowers; and although the names may be different, they are close enough to the mark to suggest that *1984*, one of the most feared political prophecies of the twentieth century, may be coming truer than we realize. While most readers picked up on the totalitarian themes, few noticed the threefold division of the world. Fiction often predates fact.

Third, issues of war and peace have not disappeared with the decline of superpower rivalry. In some ways, to be sure, the world is a safer place now than it was when the United States and the Soviet Union had huge nuclear arsenals and their policies seemed to be predicated on the bizarre and crazy assumption that nuclear holocaust was an acceptable piece of military strategy. That scenario has disappeared. But nuclear arsenals still exist, nuclear proliferation is increasing, and now almost a dozen countries have the capacity to produce nuclear weapons, not all of them bastions of freedom and democracy. The bipolar world had a kind of mad stability while the new world order has a dangerous degree of instability and anarchy. The peace movement of the 1980s was influential in shifting world opinion. Contemporary peace activists have a more difficult job: to persuade public opinion that the world is still a dangerous place, in some cases more dangerous, and that as long as states continue to pursue policy objectives through military means then war, destruction, and death will continue to threaten the globe.

For over forty years after the ending of the Second World War, the military posture of the world was crystallized into superpower rivalry. The world's arsenals were bound together into a simple, if suicidal, posture. The collapse of the Soviet Union and the decline of the cold war has acted like a solvent destroying the cozy cohesion of the world's military. The world has fractured into many different splinters, there are now many more us's and them's, and the possibilities for military engagement has increased. It is no longer the single massive threat of a superpower but the proliferation of nuclear weaponry and the fracturing of alliances that still make the world an unsafe abode. The cold war has turned into the hot peace.

The Global Economy

The *new world order* has many connotations; one of the most frequently noted is the notion of a global economy. We should be careful of this term if only applied to recent events. A convincing case can be made that ever since the sixteenth century we have been living in a global economy. Since the European appropriation of the New World, intercontinental trading patterns have been created, maintained and reinforced. For centuries commodities have been bought and sold around the world, local economies have been connected to world trading circuits and national economies have been interconnected. The global economy has a long history, one that predates the recent use of the term.

However, the increased use of the term *global economy* indicates some important changes. Let me comment on two in particular. The first is the liberalization of money from national control.

Although commodities were bought and sold around the world since the sixteenth century, finance markets tended to be national in origin. There were flows of money around the world but financial transactions had to be negotiated through the maze of national currency regulations. One of the most significant changes in recent decades had been the liberation of financial markets and the decline of national control over money flows. Smaller, weaker countries have always been subject to outside financial power; but the most interesting change in recent years has been how even the largest countries are now subject to "the market." In national politics more emphasis is given to sending the right signals to the financial markets because flights of capital can affect national stability. The rhetoric of the recent use of the term *global economy* is primarily tied to the practice of global money flows driven by relative rates of return and less subject to national systems of regulation in even the largest economies. Money has achieved its transcendent capitalist potential of even being transnational, nonnational, truly international.

The second point concerns the effect of the global economy on the economies of the strongest national economies. A global trading economy has been around for close to five hundred years. But for the past one hundred and fifty years, skilled workers in the rich countries could achieve relatively affluent lifestyles. The aristocracy of labor in the rich world benefited from the world economy. National wage-rate differences were substantially different between rich and poor world countries. The workers in the rich countries were insulated by their collective power and comparative advantage in producing value-added goods and services. In recent years there has been the global shift of manufacturing, so that what could only be done in the so-called advanced countries can now be done just as well but much cheaper in the poorer countries. With the decline of national regulation systems and the global shift of manufacturing, workers in the rich countries now have to compete directly. The result has been a downward pressure on wages in the rich countries. The global economy now involves the direct competition between low- and high-wage economies with, given the nature of relatively free global trade, a decline in the high-wage rates of the richer economies. The term *global economy* refers not so much to the integration of the world economy, a trend that has long historical roots, but more to the direct economic competition faced by the workers of the advanced countries. The labor aristocracy of the rich world now has to compete more in the global economy and benefits less.

The current use of the term global economy refers to the interantionalization of money and wage-rate competition. There has been political fallout. The decline of living standards has provoked bouts of economic populism in some countries such as the United States. It has caused a reassessment of the power and direction of the nation-state. Even the more powerful states have difficulty in resisting the pressures of global competition and seem less able to secure economic benefits for its citizenry.

The current global economy has superimposed the rapid flows of money and global wage competition over the centuries old world trading patterns. The costs and benefits have varied across the world. In many formerly poor countries, manufacturing employment has created a new proletariat. The old peasantry has been turned into industrial-urban workers. In the richer countries' wage, there has been a decline in the power and size of the traditional working class. In the United States, given its more elastic use of class terms, it is seen as the decline of the middle class. There is a global reorganization in which the industrial workforce is being transformed around the world. In this transitional period, the gains of the old working class organizations are being lost, and the new proletariat has yet to organize.

The Global Village

The term *new world order* has also been used to denote a more interconnected world. And there is some truth to this. The world has become a smaller place, and the change is comparatively recent. Even as late as the nineteenth century, there were still areas of the world described as terra incognito, blank spaces waiting to be filled. They were not empty. People lived there, but from the supreme arrogance of a white Eurocentric perspective, they were seen as savages living in a wilderness. As we near the end of the twentieth century there are no empty spaces left. The great explorations are over. The Columbus and Magellan of the contemporary period are the Einsteins and Freuds, people who uncovered new worlds at the level of subatomic particles or found undiscovered lands below the level of our everyday consciousness.

Although the dimensions of the planet have remained the same, the world has become smaller. In two respects. Improvements in transport have shrunk the world in space-time. In 1873 *Around the World in Eighty Days* was first published. Jules Verne's novel was an adventure story suited to the transport capabilities of its time. Now it would take less than eighty hours to travel around the world by commercial airline.

The world is closer together than it ever was. This closeness is a function of not only transport improvements but also advancements in telecommunications. The world is closer because we now know more about what happens in other parts of it. Radio, television, telephones, faxes, and satellites have brought us closer together. Not everyone has equal access to the means of communication, some parts of the world are better covered than others, and information is filtered through the lens of bias and driven by a commercial imperative. Despite these qualifications there is more readily available information about other parts of the world. In 1964, Marshall McLuhan suggested that we live in a global village. A long-term perspective would seem to validate his hypothesis. It took over six weeks before most people in Britain knew about the Battle of Trafalgar (1805) but less than six hours for most people to hear of the latest reports from fighting in the Falklands in 1982. Around the world many people remember where they were when they heard of the assassination of President Kennedy in 1963. The tragic event seared the time and place on many a memory. The television in our sitting room gives us coverage of events from around the world as they happen. The world has shrunk in size to a more intimate place. Whenever there is a coup or a counterrevolution, the first thing people do is try to capture the radio and television stations. Those who control the means of communication wield immense power, influencing public opinion at home and abroad. And whenever repressive regimes do evil against their populations, they seek a ban on impartial news coverage. A new and powerful force has been created in the global village—the force of world public opinion, a force with powerful effects on world events. Coverage of battles makes it difficult for states to ignore the bloody costs of warfare. When East Germans demonstrated in Leipzig against the Communist regime, their resistance was seen all over the world; and in Czechoslovakia and Rumania it became a source of hope and inspiration in the struggle against oppression. The coverage of events affects the course of events. It is very unlikely that Nelson Mandela would ever have survived a South African prison let alone be released if it was not for the unblinking gaze of world opinion. One important element in the new world order, and one that is genuinely new, is the greater role for public opinion. This opinion is massaged and contorted by the mass media with their bias and predilections. Not every social problem becomes an issue, not every issue reaches the political agenda, and not all items on this agenda receive equal treatment. We could spend a great deal of time noting the operation of bias, but what is important at this stage is to note the presence of this opinion, no matter how flawed, as an indicator of general feelings. And international public opinion has been mobilized by such organizations as Amnesty, which throw a light on some of the darkest secrets of the state against the people.

A global perspective is represented in art and literature. In response to the claim that the novel was dead, Salman Rushdie argued:

> Might it not be simply that a new novel is emerging—a postcolonial novel, a decentered, transnational, interlingual, crosscultural novel—and that in this new world order or disorder, we find a better explanation of the contemporary novel's health (Rushdie 1996, 55).

Rushdie's own novels, especially *Midnight's Children*, represent a fine example of such a new novel.

Our perception of the world very much depends upon the pictures we have of the earth. The famous photographs from the Apollo mission, which show the earth as a small, fragile ball floating in the inky blackness of deep space, have become a powerful image and an arresting metaphor. It is not accidental that, soon after the pictures appeared in 1969, the first Earth Day was commemorated in April 1970. The notion of the earth as a single entity has fueled causes of one-worldism and aided perceptions of "Spaceship Earth" as an interdependent, fragile ecosystem.

There is now a greater sense of the interconnectedness of the world. As our technological ability has grown and our world has "shrunk," we have become more aware of the global impacts of "local" events. When a nuclear power station in Russia blows up, the radioactive dust pollutes the uplands in north Wales and the Lake District of England; smoke from chimneys in China affects the amount of sunlight in North America; and the felling of trees in Amazonia reduces the amount of oxygen for everyone in the world. The shrinking of the world is a function of our interdependence. What happens in one part of the global village affects all the other parts. And with this knowledge comes an awareness of the fragility of our occupancy of the planet and for many a sense of responsibility about the future. More than any other generation before us, the fear of the future lies heavy on our shoulders.

In the last century, the dominant view of the world was from the well-appointed offices and homes of the rich elite in the powerful countries of Europe and North America. The world was a space to be occupied, transformed, incorporated into a world economy and a "civilized" discourse. Knowledge was provided for them and by them. Their narrow attitudes and specific tastes were seen as universal standards of knowledge and culture. An alternative perspective to emerge in the last third of the twentieth century and encapsulated in those beautiful pictures of the earth from distant satellites is of a tiny planet with life precariously balanced on its surface, a small globe in a vast universe, home to a population bound together by news and information, economic transactions, and a shared occupancy of a fragile ecosystem. At the end of the second millennium, we have discovered that the world is a very small place. Perhaps that is the greatest geographical discovery.

For the global villagers of the new millenium, there are a number of causes of concern as well as sources of optimism. One of the most important is the increasing awareness of the fundamental importance of environmental issues. These environmental issues have always been discussed. There was the strengthening of the environmental movement in the late 1960s and early 1970s, but the world recession of 1974 shifted attention to issues of economic growth. In the 1980s a revival of significant interest in environmental issues occurred, which, I think, will be of lasting importance. The concern with the environment is no longer the preserve of middle-class intellectuals in the affluent suburbs of the rich world; it goes wider and deeper. It links people across the world. There is now an awareness that what happens in one part of the globe, be it the burning of the rain forest, an explosion at a nuclear power plant, or the emission of car exhaust fumes, has a direct impact on all the other parts. There is a web of ecological processes that makes us dependent on the natural resources of the world and on the actions of fellow global villagers. There is now a whole series of issues—protecting the rain forest, maintaining ecological diversity, and ensuring the continued livability of the planet—that transcends national boundaries and the concerns of just the rich world. There is an acceptance of the tremendous importance of the ecological balance between the human and the natural world; this realization will inform world debates and national politics for many years to come. The politics of environmental concern will become a dominant movement at the global, national, and local level. Green politics will be allied to a range of other concerns, including the women's movement, the pacifist movement, and the rights of indigenous peoples. A whole set of concerns will cluster around and find coherence in the notion of environmentalism. The questioning of economic growth as a national priority, quality of life issues, and the concern with leading a dignified, sustainable life for all will be addressed in and through the environmental question.

For the global villagers, the struggle over the meaning of environment is the new metanarrative. Green geopolitics has become the new universal discourse. At the global level, there is the contest for the earth to be a safe, toxic-free environment for the nurturing of human life. At the local level is the concern with the quality of life in particular places. Ranged against these concerns are mighty forces of political and economic power. At the heart of the new world order is a struggle for the meaning of place.

The world is in flux. Old empires are falling, new states are emerging. There is a sense of profound change. The past no longer provides us with a secure guide to the future, and even the present is difficult to comprehend. At times like these we should consider our knowledge provisional and limited, with much of it based on events and structures that no longer have relevance. But the recent past can teach us something. The lessons of the late 1980s? A sense of humility as even the securest foundations of the world order were swept aside and a reaffirmation of the important role for ordinary people to change structures and influence events. These are profound lessons to take into the next millenium.

2

The State and the New World Order

The state is the point of connection between the world order and the lives of ordinary people. The state links the global economy with the household economy, the generality of world order with the particularity of individual households. The state mediates between the global and the local, space and place, the long term with the short run.

In this chapter I want to consider three important elements in the relationship between the state and the new world order: the paradox of the state, the nation and the state, and the social contract.

The Paradox of the State

The essential paradox of the state in the new world order is that the state is, at the same time, too small and too big.

Too Small

In an era of transnational capitalism, global flows of capital, and an integrated world economy the state appears impotent. Small states have always been at the mercy of larger powers, but the creation of a global marketplace has rendered weak even the power of the largest states. The government of the United States, for example, is unable to stop the fall in the standard of living of its citizenry that has occurred in the past twenty years. Individual states find it difficult, on their own, to buck the "market," halt flights of capital, or attract inward investment.

There is also the fact that the states is too small a unit to cope with ecological issues that respect neither national boundaries nor states authority.

In effect, the state is too small because the global economy has weakened the power of the individual state and the most pressing concerns require global solutions. Ecological problems know no frontiers, and contemporary capitalism is a world system where investment and disinvestment range across the globe. The workings of the natural environment and the world economy pay scant respect to national boundaries.

There have always been some states that wield very little power. The distinction between superpowers, major powers and minor powers, indicates the nature of the hierarchy. There is a world of difference in the power available to the United States, Lesotho, or Peru. There have always been inequalities. What is more recent is the extent to which even the largest and most powerful states are increasingly unable to influence events on their own. Take the case of the United States. It is the largest single military power, but its economic power is threatened by a strong Japan and an emerging Europe and its international policings are subject to international approval and disapproval; the United Nations is no longer the rubber stamp to US actions it used to be. The United Nations still tends to support the United States, but in recent years there have been stirrings of a more independent line. And even in the United States, the imperative of corporate profitability is causing the shift of industry overseas and the loss of domestic manufacturing employment. To live in a global economy is to be affected by global competition, even for the strongest states.

The richest countries are also tied into the web of ecological dependency. The burning of the rain forest, the release of chemicals into the atmosphere, the pollution of the soil and seas all impinge on the quality of life of all societies, including the most affluent. The solution to these problems also lies beyond the narrow confines of the largest states.

There are two responses. The first, connected with economic considerations, is to seek the safety of larger groupings. This is the "bloc" solution. Small countries have always banded together with larger countries for increased safety and security. But in the global village, even the largest countries need the reassurance of others. The North American Free Trade Agreement between Canada, the United States, and Mexico is one such attempt to provide a larger internal market than each country can provide on its own. The European Community is one of the most successful groupings. A main reason behind its initial establishment was to tie Germany into a broader grouping and avoid the resurgence of German nationalism. The strategy has been successful. Postwar enmities were buried by economic ties as former enemies became economic allies. It is now inconceivable to think of a war between Western European powers. But for the first half of the twentieth century conflict between these countries engulfed the world in total war. That is no longer a legitimate fear, and it has occurred because a pan-Europeanism, although not replacing nationalism, has at the very least softened its sharpest edges.

Economic conflict has been displaced to a broader level. The context for European cooperation is increased conflict with other trading blocs. As the links between France, Germany, and Italy have increased, the conflicts between the European Community and the United States and Japan have increased and are likely to increase with the disappearance of the Soviet threat. One of the problems of the new world order is to contain this economic competition so that it does not spill over into military conflict.

The second response has been greater use of international forums and organizations. This is the "international talk-shop" solution. The United Nations is increasingly used as a peacekeeper, an influential arbiter, and a potential solver of national disputes and conflicts. Countries vary in the amount of power they can wield in international forums. The United Nations, while giving almost every country a voice, still reflects the inequality of national power; and this is seen, for example, in the permanent members of the Security Council, which include the United States, the United Kingdom, Russia, France and China. The United States picks up the tab for almost one-third of the United Nation's peacekeeping costs and is the biggest single contributor to the budget of the myriad agencies of the organization. Other international agencies, such as the World Bank and the International Monetary Fund (IMF), display a similar pattern of equal membership but unfair distribution in terms of funding and the consequent ability to influence outcomes. After the Second World War, many international organizations were established, including the United Nations, the World Bank, and IMF. In effect, however, they codified, reinforced, and legitimized Western dominance and US hegemony. In the intervening years, the international organizations have opened up to a wider range of opinions and perspectives. Despite US protestations, for example, the United Nations has had a more pro-Arab and anti-Israel stance than that of the United States. On the one hand, the richer countries, and particularly the United States, pay for the upkeep of international organizations; but on the other, even the richest countries need international approval. To maintain their power, the dominant countries need to control international organizations; but to maintain some measure of consensus, they also need to give some semblance of equal representation. The difficult balancing act for the more powerful countries is to be in control but not to appear so. For the weaker countries, the aim is to use these international forums to gain greater control over world events. Most of the international organizations were established to reinforce the distribution of power, but the forums have provided the many more smaller countries the opportunity to influence outcomes.

The major weakness of international forums and organizations is the self-imposed limits on their jurisdiction and powers. No state wants to give up its power and sovereignty to an international organization. There is a pressing need for a global perspective, but few states want to give up their power. The British government supports UN peacekeeping forces in Cambodia but is reluctant to see the United Nations get involved in Northern Ireland. The United States wants sanctions imposed on certain "aggressive" actions, such as the Iraqi invasion of Kuwait, but wants to be able to invade Panama. Japan is a signatory to species preservation measures but does little to stop its own fishing industry from overfishing the stocks of tuna and whale. Many poorer countries and less powerful states see some measure of hypocrisy in these actions. In March 1992, for example, at the Convention of International Trade in Endangered Species (CITES) five African nations suggested a ban on the trade of the Atlantic herring. It was an attempt to make a serious point. The European and North American states found it easier to get worked up about the need for bans on African elephants but failed to do much about the ecological problems on their own doorstep.

It is appropriate, at this stage, to introduce my "law of moral outrage." This law, which covers civil rights, ecological matters, and matters of political principle, states that the level of moral outrage that a country expresses about an issue is in direct proportion to the distance between that country and the issue in question. The greater the distance, the greater the sense of outrage. European powers get more upset about the burning of the Brazilian rain forest, for example, than they do about the destruction of natural habitats within their own national boundaries. In the United States, more moral outrage is expressed about racism in South Africa than about racism in the United States. Distance lends the benefit of certainty, the easy assurance of the right answer to a simple problem. This is not to make the easy charge of hypocrisy. Very often, the distant perspective is clearer and gets right to the heart of the matter . . . and right to the solution. The rich countries involved in CITES, for example, were making an important point about the endangered status of the African elephant. In 1970 there were 2.5 million elephants, but by 1992 estimates ranged from 350,000 to 600,000. Whatever estimate is taken, the figures indicate a dramatic decline. Just because faraway countries make a point does not invalidate that point.

International organizations still reflect the balance of power rather than the power of rational argument; international sanctions and prescriptions are thus easier to impose on the poorer countries of the world. Indeed "international" issues are very often defined as those that relate to the weaker countries. International opinion is more difficult to mobilize against the richer countries. Thus CITES found it easier to impose limits on trade in ivory than it did on the proposal to limit restrictions on the killing of North American black bears. Each species is equally endangered, but the one living in poorer countries is more susceptible to international opinion and intervention.

The major problems and issues that face us are global problems and world issues. Economic growth, environmental degradation, the fear of war, the obscenity of starving children—these are all things that can only be resolved through international action and cooperation. A global society has been created, but a global community has proved more difficult to achieve. The bloc solution provides a way out for the individual state but can create economic conflict with other blocs while the international talk-shop solution has self-imposed constraints. There is an optimistic conclusion and a pessimistic conclusion. The pessimist will suggest that competition between the giant economic blocs will develop into military conflict and that international forums are just the more benign form of neoimperialism by which the rich world still controls the poor world. The optimist, in contrast, will argue that the big blocs and the international organizations are merely the transitional forms, compromised and flawed, but still the right steps in the direction of a fairer, safer, global community. Only time, as they say, will tell.

Too Large

One of the most significant trends of the twentieth century has been the enlargement and consolidation of the power of the state. Throughout the world civil society has been incorporated, enmeshed, and in some instances replaced by government. There has been a bureaucratization and a politicization of public and private life. This has occurred even in societies where individual freedoms are enshrined as political rights. The net effect is to make the state too big.

In many societies there is no countervailing political power to the state. Economic power rests with corporations and the power of capital, but political power resides within and through the state. Between the power of big capital and big government, the individual citizen, the local community, and the small neighborhood have little power or influence. There has been a spiral of incorporation as movements, organizations, and institutions are woven into the texture of state power. The result is the incorporation of myriad interests, varied concerns, and different practices into the more uniform language and practice of big government.

There has been a decline in the power and significance of civil society. Sometimes for the good. In its more benign forms, the state can do much to ameliorate the excesses and inequalities of the market. In many rich countries, the experience of poverty is softened by redistributional policies. But one of the consequences has been the loss of civic obligations as an important principle. We have got so used to interacting with each other in and through the state that we have lost the language and experience of direct social interaction. That is what I mean by the decline of civil society. The extension of the state into so many areas of our lives has given great social advances, but it has also weakened our capacity and ability to be active citizens as opposed to passive voters. This position needs care in its exposition as it is easy to slip into a justification of the status quo whereby the poor in rich countries are cared for only by the charity of private individuals. We can ask for more obligations in civil society without abrogating the caring role of the state.

The more powerful politicians become, the more distant they are from the life and experience of ordinary people. They are screened from everyday concerns, are isolated from local communities, and interact with the citizenry only in symbolic theatrical photo opportunities. In democracies there is always the power of the ballot. But while the ballot can reflect political choice, it rarely reflects power. Power does not reside in choosing this or that politician but in funding campaigns, informing the agenda, and generating the winds of political and economic power in which all politicians have to steer a course.

At its most awkward, the state is too small to address global issues yet too big to respond to local concerns. The state is too parochial to meet the needs of a global community yet too big and distant to meet the requirements of a local community. The state will continue to exist—where else can politicians go and what else can they do?—but as a source of emancipatory change, the single state is becoming more and more irrelevant. Throughout most of the century, the state has been seen as the point of emancipatory contact between civil society, the market, and political culture. For the first two-thirds of the twentieth century, for example, the aim of many British socialists was to capture the "commanding heights" of the national economy. It was an enterprise suited to its time. It was a national, top-down view of social change that could more easily ignore the international dimension and community participation. It is easy to criticize this attitude as well as its failures. Too easy. Rather, let us note the way the world has changed. The commanding heights are no longer at the national level, and a top-down vision of social reform has many flaws. At the end of the twentieth century, it is more and more apparent that pressing issues of social justice, environmental quality, and the construction of a humane economy should be addressed not only at the level of the state. For the radicals of the new world order, the commanding heights include not only the existing power within the state but the international forums, the giant economic blocs as well as the local communities. "Act locally, think globally" is a neat but limiting phrase. More useful, though much less punchy, is "Act globally, act nationally, act locally."

The Nation and the State

We can make a distinction between nation and state. A nation is a group of people with a perceived shared identity and attachment to particular parts of the land; a nation has a history and a geography. The state, on the other hand, is an administrative-political-spatial entity. Where the boundaries of the nation and the state coincide, there is little strain. Tensions arise when and where perceived national boundaries cross state boundaries.

In many parts of the world, there is still a mismatch between the boundaries of the state and the national allegiance of the people. We can identify a number of different circumstances. Nations without states continue to be a source of tension. The case of Palestine is the most obvious and one of the most pressing; but the Kurds, the Basques, the Scots, and numerous other nations without states give cause for concern. These are the disenfranchised of the political world. In 1991 the Unrepresented Nations and Peoples' Organization claimed thirty-nine members, covering 130 million people. It is in the nature of all organizations to inflate their membership. But even with this fact in mind, the figures suggest a significant proportion of the world's population.

Then there are the states with more than one nation. There are only a few cases where the boundaries of the state and national identity are in perfect synchronization. Even in the relatively stable countries, there are mismatches. In Britain, Scots and Welsh nationalism is like a fire in the basement, little seen and rarely attended to until it gets out of control. Northern Ireland shows what happens when things get out of control. In the United States the concept of a republic indivisible is being questioned. The motto of the Republic *E pluribus unum* (One from the many) is being challenged. Some African-American intellectuals repeat the notion of some form of separation from the white establishment, and debates over language and religious teaching continue to stretch the discourse of the state over a number of emerging "nations." One report for the New York State Education Commissioner in 1989 was entitled "One Nation, Many Peoples."

Throughout much of the world, individual states contain more than one nation. Often they exist in an uneasy tension, and occasionally the tensions flare into civil war. In the early 1990s, the former Yugoslavia fractured into constituent republics, and ethnic tensions between Croats, Serbs, and Muslims in Croatia and Bosnia dominated the news headlines and world political attention. In many parts of the world, there is still a mismatch between the boundaries of the state and those of the nation. The continual drive to national expression provides a source of major political change in the world. As long as state boundaries fail to express national identities, there will be a source of dispute between the population and the state.

Throughout most of the twentieth century it was assumed by many that nationalism was an old-fashioned concept with little place in the modern world. Indeed, there were whole ideologies and political movements—socialism and communism being the most important and persuasive—that were ostensibly based on the end of nationalism and the demise of the parochial and limited interests of the contemporary state. Nationalism, however, has proved to be more resilient. More than that it seems to be growing. The renewal of the nationalist enterprise is part of a broader shift. A postmodern world is one where identity is based on a hierarchy of levels, not just the global as with the modernist conception, but global *and* national *and* local; not just with the forward march of history, space, and universals, but particular identities, place, and local knowledges.

Old Nationalisms in the "New" World

In America and Australia, European powers subjugated and marginalized the indigenous people. While intellectuals swayed between conceptions of Noble and Ignoble Savage, the practitioners of power created the Powerless Savage. In North America, South America, and Australia the indigenous people were stripped of much of their land, culture, and dignity. At the high point of Victorian triumphalism, they were seen as remnants of an inferior culture, soon to displaced completely by a stronger society. The operation of "survival of the fittest" would leave them with neither space nor role in modern society.

These people proved more tenacious than the predictions of the social Darwinists. Weakened and sometimes dispirited, the Australian aborigines, native North Americans, and the people of the South American forest hung on. By the end of the twentieth century, there was a profound change of attitude—on both sides. The indigenous people were increasingly seen by many non-indigenous groups as keepers of a special wisdom, living testaments to the power of resistance against the modern world and role models for a more ecological lifestyle. They became praised rather than criticized, celebrated rather than marginalized. The indigenous presence was felt in the celebrations of national identity. In 1988 white Australia celebrated its bicentennial. Two hundred years earlier, an antipodean gulag was established by the British. The celebrations were resisted by aborigines, whose presence and protestations brought into sharp relief the dark side of white celebrations. Similarly, in 1992 there were celebrations in the United States for the five-hundred-year anniversary of the landing of Columbus. Native American activists argued that there was nothing to celebrate because the coming of Columbus was the beginning of their defeat; it inaugurated a time of cultural genocide. The celebrations, unlike the celebrations one hundred years earlier, became sites of resistance, acts of different rememberings, alternative histories, and competing narratives.

These indigenous nationalisms focus on cultural resistance. In some cases this is bound up with the concept of land rights, laying claim to land no longer thought to belong to the indigenous people. In Australia and throughout North America, land claims, ranging from the purely symbolic to the very possible, reflect and condense this new nationalism. This "new" nationalism is not a nationalism of a separate state but the nationalism of continued resistance.

Old Nationalisms in the New Europe

In Eastern Europe nationalism was and is exacerbated by the particular circumstance of the decline of Soviet power and the demise of the Communist system. The end of the cold war and that decline of Soviet power has removed the glue from the multinational states of Eastern Europe. Before these momentous changes, separatist movements could be portrayed by state authorities as anti-Communist, subversive activities. And given the ideology of communism—the belief in world citizenship and the emphasis on class divisions rather than ethnic identity—there was little space for the expression of national separatism. Moreover, the decline of Communist hegemony undermined the legitimacy of the state, its former leaders, and its present boundaries. Many of these states, as elsewhere in the world, were compromises owing more to postwar deals than to authentic nationalist sentiment. The delegitimizing of the Communist state affected popular attitudes toward the state. With the decline of communism, everything associated with the former regimes was questioned and reevaluated, including the boundaries of the state:

boundaries in the double sense of limitations on state activity and the territorial distribution of the state.

Nationalism continues to exercise the popular imagination and provides an important vehicle for the mobilization of popular protest. We can see two processes in operation. There are the centrifugal forces that are prizing apart multinational states. Yugoslavia is the most obvious as the former Communist state is fracturing along the fault lines of Serbia, Croatia, and the other constituent elements and deepening centuries-old ethnic tension and conflict. Then there are the centripetal movements as ethnic groups separated by state boundaries seek some form of alliance. The exemplar case here is of the unified Germany that has healed the division between East and West, a process that may not be over. German-speaking peoples can still be found in Poland and in the Czech Republic.

Tom Nairn has referred to nationalism as having a Janus-faced quality, which looks to both the past and the present (Nairn 1977, 1–3). The reemergence of nationalism is a response that captures past loyalties and present-day economic realities. The look back at the past is part of a broader move, the shift from modern to postmodern, the move away from a belief in universals to a concern with the particular, the local, the vernacular. It is a concern with locality, an interest more in place than space. Socialism was a belief in the universal, the general, space rather than place, the forward march of history rather than the ties that bind us to the past. The demise of socialism is part of the jettisoning of belief in universal progress. We have retreated from supranational concerns and rediscovered national uniqueness. Renewed nationalist sentiments are part of this rediscovery. But it is not a complete rejection of a global perspective. Indeed, the paradox is that, in many parts of the world, nationalist sentiment is flourishing because of the increasingly global nature of economic transactions, social trends, and ecological concerns. The boundaries of many, if not all, states look more and more irrelevant when set against the emergence of the global village. In Europe the creation and strengthening of the EEC has allowed nationalist movements to gain confidence because a new supranational entity bypasses the old authority of the states and allows old nationalist regions to exist. When Brussels becomes the center of a new European state, then the Scots will no longer need to pay allegiance to London.

To every action there is an historical reaction. We have abandoned the belief in the universal citizen permanently looking forward to the progress of history. The idea may still be appealing, but it has been polluted by the reality of the attempt. The reaction is a return to older loyalties, blood ties, and territorial connections. All social movements contain both positive and negative qualities. After the dangers of centralized political power have been exposed, it is as well to think again of the dangers of nationalism. Nationalism is concerned with celebrating and expressing the nation, but this involves a distinction between nation and nonnation, us and them. If the twentieth-century history of Europe has taught us anything, it is surely the inherent dangers of such designations.

The Social Contract

The relationship between the state and the citizenry has long been a central focus of political thought. The term *social contract* is often used to refer to this relationship. The best contract is an agreement between the state and the people that allows the state to govern and the people to live freely. The agreement is breached by the government when it suspends rights and imprisons and unfairly treats all or parts of the population. In this section I want to make three remarks about the social contract and the new world order; in particular I want to examine the notion of political freedom and rights, majority rule and minority rights, and the distinction between rights and obligations.

Freedom and Rights

We should be wary of the easy assumption that the fall of communism in the former Soviet Empire will by itself increase political freedoms. We have to question the assumption that "free" markets produce free peoples. Although the demise of central planning will involve a freeing of markets, there is no one-to-one relationship between the workings of the marketplace and the creation and maintenance of political freedoms. The assumption is too often made that capitalism, in the form of the operation of private markets, is inimical to the freedoms and rights associated with liberal democracies. Capitalism is an economic system that can survive and prosper in a variety of political contexts, from liberal democracies to fascist dictatorships. Just because capitalism is dominant in the liberal democracies does not mean that there is a necessary one-to-one relationship between capitalism and the workings of liberal democracies. The operation of the marketplace neither inaugurates nor guarantees political freedoms. Indeed, a convincing argument could be drawn that the fall of communism will in the short to medium term, if not longer, cause extreme social tensions. The removal of central planning mechanisms will mean the disappearance of all kinds of social subsidies, including cheap food, accommodation, transport, and medical care. The most obvious effects of the reintroduction of full market systems will exacerbate inequalities. The citizens of much of Eastern Europe will loose the disadvantages of the Communist system before feeling the positive effects of the capitalist system.

And in the longer term, even if the advantages of the capitalist system begin to percolate throughout the new societies, there is still the issue of what rights are being secured. Classic liberal theory was predicated on the needs of property-owning individuals. The concern with rights in the political philosophy of classic liberalism is primarily the concern with protecting property rights. In both the capitalist and former Communist countries, the bias toward property rights, often to the exclusion of other rights, is being both tested and contested. The concentration on property rights as the primary rights favors property owners rather than nonproperty owners. The securing and prioritizing of property rights has distinct, regressive features. These are most apparent in the former Communist countries because of the legacy of social subsidies.

There is an increased awareness that a variety of rights can be identified. We can extend the list from life, liberty, and the pursuit of happiness to include economic rights, which assert the right to a living wage and economic security; ecological rights, to a safe humane environment; social rights, to social justice and cultural expression; and political rights, which ensure free and equal access to centers of political power. These alternative rights have yet to receive as a full theoretical elaboration as property rights, and they have still to be as tested as property rights have been in the crucible of political debate, legislative amendments, and judicial scrutiny. Yet, some of the changes of the new world order are causing a reassessment of the debate on rights.

In 1992 over two thousand Russians were asked whether they agreed with the statement "Marxism is bankrupt." Only 11 percent disagreed, whereas 46 percent agreed with the statement. But when asked if "only capitalism can save our country" only 19 percent agreed, while 44 percent disagreed. In other words although Marxism was dead, the free market was not seen as a panacea. In 1993 two thousand Russians were asked to respond to the statement "The state should provide everyone with a job and never tolerate unemployment"; 77 percent either fully agreed or rather agreed. Only 7 percent fully disagreed (Erlanger 1993, E1, E5). Too much can be taken from opinion polls, subject as they are to problems of interpretation and volatility; but these two separate studies and one of them from the conservative Radio Free Europe/Radio Liberty Research Institute, indicate that the legacy of economic justice is not so easily jettisoned as central planning or one-party states. On one side of the former iron curtain, the rights narrowly defined by classical liberalism are not the only points of political debate. Similarly, on the other side of the former iron curtain, the end of the cold war is allowing the area of political discourse to be extended. While the Russians were wanting some measure of economic justice, a significant proportion of people in the United States wanted the state to do more than just allow the operation of the "free" market. The election of Clinton in 1992 marked a change in US politics. For the first time in over a generation, a president was elected who spoke about government involvement in economic affairs, more money for domestic programs, and the necessity of major health care reforms. The thawing of the cold war has halted the fossilization of political debate and the polarization of attitudes—on both sides. And in this new terrain, the notion of rights is being extended beyond the narrow confines of protecting property interests.

Majority Rule and Minority Rights

It is a central tenet of democratic theory that majority rule is good. If a majority of people agree with a particular policy, then that is the preferred policy. Though there is a need for some checks and balances, hence the diffusion of federal power in the United States among the presidency, the Congress, and the Supreme

Court, the point of political representation is to express the majority will of the people. The new world order has brought the question of minority rights into sharp relief. Democratic theory, at least as an indicator of a just society, breaks down when the majority can and do exploit a minority. This can take a number of forms. One of the most obvious is when the renewed bouts of nationalism, especially in states with more than one nation and particularly when there is a minority nation. The so-called ethnic cleansing of Muslims in the Serbian-controlled parts of Bosnia in 1992–93 was the most dramatic expression of the oppression of minorities. The problem in multinational states is how to ensure the rights of the minority. In the worst cases where religious, ethnic, or national tensions are severe, the majority is unlikely to listen to the minority. In these cases the only "solution" is international involvement. I put quotation marks around the term because such solutions are neither easy nor obvious. It is all the more difficult when we have no theoretical template to guide our actions. If the minorities are in distinct districts or regions, then the constitution of the state along federal lines is a possibility. Some loose arrangement of federal units can allow different "nations" to be in one state. If, however, the minorities are dispersed throughout the majority population, with no distinctive spatial clustering, the federal arrangement of the state provides no solution. Outright oppression of minorities can be subject to international criticism and action, but this becomes difficult in the gray area between oppression and freedom. If the state has majority support, it becomes difficult for other states to intervene.

The new world order is a time of social dislocation. During all periods of social stress, the hunt is on for the scapegoat. The religious, ethnic, racial, and national minorities fill the slot of the "other," the possible source of turmoil, the reason why things are the way they are. Around the world, for example, homophobia seems to be on the increase in spite of, or perhaps because of, the more public demands for gay rights. In Europe the racial minorities have become the brunt of renewed nationalism and protofascism. Whether it be Gypsies in Germany, Algerians in France, Asians in Britain, or North Africans in Italy, there is a disturbing trend toward intolerance and racism. It is not the only response, and it is not uncontested; but it is a trend that feeds on economic recession, political uncertainty, and social dislocation. The new world order has its dark side. Social change can bring out the worst as well as the best in societies.

Rights and Obligations

Classic liberal theory is concerned with rights, with establishing a zone of security between individual citizens and the state. It is an atomized view of society. The principal concern is with protecting people from the state. This is important, necessary, and still vital in a world where the state can and does frequently impinge on basic human rights. But there is a silence. Liberal theory and practice tell us a lot about what separates us from the state as well as from each other. It says very little about what connects us, what binds us one with another as well as collectively in and through the state. Lacking such concepts we have to fall either on the market as the system that wraps us in a web of mutual self-interest or in some notion of nationality. Each of these social "cements" has its problems. Market mechanisms can and do produce inequitable outcomes, while nationalism excludes as well as includes. Elsewhere, I have described the alternative civic tradition that, stretching back to Aristotle through Rousseau, Hegel, and Marx and including Hannah Arendt, R. H. Tawney, and Michael Walzer, focuses on participation, engagement, and involvement (Short 1989). Citizenship in the civic tradition is an active engagement in the means and ends of social affairs. The problem is that the rhetoric of the civic tradition was co-opted by the Communist regimes of the former Soviet empire. This hijacking of obligations tended to stress the elaboration and defense of rights in the West. On one side of the iron curtain, the language but not the practice, of the civic tradition was employed. The Peoples Democratic Republics were rarely democratic, did not involve the people, and were not republics. On the other side, there was a strong sense of rights but a weak notion of citizen involvement. To speak of citizen obligations was to conjure up the specter of a totalitarian regime, where citizens were always within the power of the state. From *Brave New World* to *1984,* the political disutopia that was feared involved the loss of rights and the enforced performance of civic acts. The notion of obligations was tainted by the experience of Communist societies. The end of the cold war and the fall of communism provides a new opportunity for us to think about the collective as well as the individual social enterprise. It allows us the fresh opportunity to renew and revitalize the civic tradition. We already have some indications. One element in the environmental movement, for example, stresses the role and importance of individual ecological responsibility. From refusing to buy certain products, buying others, and recycling trash, the discourse of environmentalism stresses obligations more than individual rights. The question is can we transfer this discourse into the more formal political arena?

The new world in which we live is a time of pronounced political change. The state, so long the center of political debate, is being challenged by the rise of a global society and more local allegiances. It will not disappear. At least for a while. In the meantime the end of the cold war is allowing a renewed debate about the function of the state and the nature of the social contract. Questions of economic justice, ecological rights, and notions of empowerment will be contested, elaborated, and formulated in the political practice of the years ahead. Extending the notion of rights beyond the narrow definition of property and balancing rights with obligations, the individual with the state, majority rule with minority rights are all matters of pressing concern brought to life by the new geopolitics.

3

The New Urban Order

In a number of academic papers and books, I have introduced the concept of a new urban order. In this chapter I want to consider three elements of this order: cities and the global economy, new images for old cities, and the postmodern city.

Cities and the Global Economy

Cities are embedded in a world economy; they are nodes in a global network of production, consumption and exchange of commodities, goods, and services. The cities of the world make solid in time and space the nature of changing economic transactions. They are the physical embodiment of social and economic change. The changing nature of cities can tell us much about the changing nature of society.

Since the mid-1970s a new regime of capital accumulation has been identified. The term *flexible accumulation* has been used as a shorthand to refer to new labor processes, labor markets, and systems of production marked by greater flexibility and deregulation. Two major economic trends have been superimposed upon this structural transformation: first, the continued growth, at least until the early 1990s, of producer services, those knowledge-based industries of the service sector, including banking, insurance, and the full range of business services. This growth was very urban biased, especially toward the bigger world cities. Second, there were the revolutions in manufacturing. Developments in production techniques loosened the tie of manufacturing industries to centers of skilled population. Modern manufacturing became less reliant on skilled labor; mass production techniques now require less specialized labor. Improvements in transportation freed industry from traditional locations. Moreover, the sheer bulk of many goods and commodities has been substantially reduced. Compare a stereo system or video camera of even just ten years ago with the size and weight of these goods produced today. The net result of these recent technological and transport improvements is that manufacturing industries have become more efficient. Manufacturing industries need fewer people, and companies have greater flexibility in choosing the site of their operation. With everything being equal, they tend to shift to areas of low-cost labor.

At the international level, there has been a shift of industrial employment from the core countries to the semiperipheral and peripheral countries of the world economy. Peter Dicken uses the term *global shift* to refer to this change, which is caused by the ability of manufacturing companies to base their operations in a number of different locations (Dicken 1986). In effect there has been a deindustrialization, involving the decline of employment in traditional areas and an overall shift of manufacturing employment from the First World to the Third World. The consequences are most marked in those cities in the old industrial regions of mature capitalist economies that have a heavy reliance on traditional manufacturing employment. In the United States, for example, cities such as Detroit or Buffalo have experienced a real decline since the early 1970s, but even in larger cities such as Los Angeles, New York, and Chicago, which have a broader economic base, the loss of manufacturing jobs has reduced the level of higher-income, manual, male employment. The jobs that have been lost have been skilled and unskilled, traditionally male employment with a history of strong unionization. The expanding job sector, throughout the 1970s and 1980s, was the service sector with more female employment, more part-time workers and a distinct bifurcation between a core of highly paid, highly skilled, managerial-type workers and a semiperipheral and peripheral group of workers who have less attractive conditions of employment.

At the national level, the picture varies. The collective term *Third World*, for example, does not mean that all poor countries received equal amounts of manufacturing employment. The Asian "tigers" of Malaysia, South Korea, Singapore, Taiwan, and Hong Kong obtained the lion's share; and much of it provided the basis for self-sustaining growth. In Sri Lanka, by contrast, manufacturing employment is restricted to small sectors of the national economy, with most of the profits and multiplier effects exported abroad. In other countries the growth of the 1970s and 1980s laid the basis for problems in the late 1980s and 1990s. In much of Latin America, growth in the first period was predicated on heavy borrowing. With the downturn in the world economy and interest rate increases in the early 1980s, many of these countries have been faced with a debt crisis of major proportions. Responses have varied from loan defaults and cutbacks on social expenditures to a rigorous fiscal regime that badly affects the low income population. In the First, World the same story of marked variation also appears. The experience of 1980s' boom and early 1990s' slump was experienced very differently in different countries. At the two extremes are Japan and Britain. Japan experienced steady economic growth and low unemployment. The so-called bubble economy has burst, based as it was on inflating land prices and huge trade surpluses; but the economy is still in reasonable shape. In Britain, in contrast, large-scale unemployment and low growth have persisted. The boom of the 1980s was only experienced in the southeast region of the country centered on London; and with the bursting of London's bubble economy, the whole country is under the shroud of sustained economic decline. The experience of the United States falls somewhere between the two: not so much growth as in Japan but not so much decline as in Britain.

It is at the urban level that economic changes are registered most clearly. The "national" economy is something of a statistical fiction, an averaging of different urban regions. Because of the globalization of production, consumption, and exchange in association with the decline of national regulation in wage fixing and work practices, the national becomes a less significant unit of analysis. The "global" becomes more significant as the unit for understanding general economic trends, while the "urban" becomes the unit for appreciating the intersection between capital and labor, economy and society, polity and comity. London, New York, and Tokyo share more similarities with each other than they do with Glasgow, Cleveland, or Osaka respectively. At the urban level, the recent changes in the world economy vary by the size and economic base of the city.

World Cities

At the apex of the urban hierarchy, the very largest cities lost their status as manufacturing centers, and new employment growth in the 1970s and through most of the 1980s was dominated by service employment. In the world cities this resulted in a marked polarization. On the one hand, there was the growth of the yuppie; the icon of the 1980s' boom was the urban-based young professional working in the financial sector. It was always as much myth as reality, but the myth captured an important trend. On the other hand, there was the emergence of the yuffie, the young urban failure beached on the shore of indifference by the loss of manufacturing employment and the restriction of the less-educated males to service employment that paid less than a quarter of top manufacturing rates (Short 1989). The result was a dual city, rich and poor sharing the same urban space. The experience was mixed. Tokyo had fewer street people than London because the city was part of a richer society with a more even distribution of wealth. London had fewer street people than New York and they suffered less because they had better access to more welfare provisions.

The 1980s was the period of marked division between rich and poor. By the early 1990s, however, many of the yuppies had to sell their BMWs. With the slump came the cry of the middle class. Shielded from the manufacturing restructuring of the early 1980s, the downturn in the demand for producer services, and the removal of many of the middle levels of management, the yuppies were replaced by the mids, middle-incomes in distress. Again, the experience varied. In the United States, loss of employment can mean loss of health insurance coverage, inability to pay college fees, and a quick drop into the less than affluent. In Japan corporate culture dictates fewer firings, whereas in Britain the very worst effects of unemployment are softened by universal health care and income-support schemes.

Boom Cities

Below the level of world cities are the regional and national capitals. Examples include Bristol in England, Seattle and Atlanta in the United States, Bordeaux in France, and Bologna in Italy. Here, the loss of manufacturing was sometimes offset by the growth of producer services, both public and private services, including financial, government, health care, and education. In these cities there was never the same polarization as there was in the world cities, and in the 1980s some of these cities experienced some of the largest growth in the First World. Greatest growth was experienced by amenity-rich cities on the fringes of economically buoyant urban regions: for example, Silicon Valley next to San Francisco and Reading close to London. But even here the downturn of the world economy in the early 1990s led to changed expectations. The benign cycle of growth attracting investment generating new growth was broken by the economic downswing. It will be interesting to see how the boom towns of the 1980s will respond to the changed economic climate of the early twenty-first century.

The most obvious boom cities of the world were in the Third World, where rates of growth, fueled by both natural increase and a high level of rural-urban migration, bordered on the spectacular. Of the twenty-five cities expected to exceed 10 million people by the end of this century, eighteen of them will be in the Third World. Mexico City, for example, had a population of 5 million in 1950. By 1990 it had increased to 16 million, and the estimates for 2000 suggest 25 million. In these cities we can speak about urban explosion without much economic growth. The population growth of these cities is based on an urban primacy where individual cities contain the bulk of national investment, economic growth and political power, and on the lack of alternatives. Living in the city provides access to employment, formal and informal, and a range of public and private services that are unavailable to the rural dweller. The cities are a magnet, not an attractive magnet but one often providing a marginally better opportunity for the rural poor than can be found staying where they are. There is something about moving that bespeaks effort, trying to make something better of your life. The great tide of rural to urban migration is fueled by the waves of human hope. It is as well to remember this when the focus is only on the slums and shantytowns, the crime and the pollution. There is a superior Western academic attitude that looks only to the problems of these booming cities. And there are problems aplenty: urban infrastructure overwhelmed by the population explosion, lack of high-paid employment, pollution, and lack of affordable shelter. But there are also glimmers of light. The self-help construction of housing, creation of an informal economy, and recycling of goods and materials derive from hardship; but they also represent human ingenuity as well as market failures, solutions as well as problems.

Slump Cities

There is urban decline around the world as well as urban growth. In the richer world, the most rapid decline has occurred in old manufacturing centers. In cities where the economic base is overwhelmingly manufacturing, the decline has not been offset by an increase in producer services. In medium-sized cities without national or regional capital functions, for example, Buffalo, New York, or Glasgow, Scotland, manufacturing decline can be expressed as net decline. There is a loss not only of jobs but of the defining spirit of these places, built as they were on a culture of blue-collar employment.

The experience of decline varies by size. There is something called the urban ratchet effect. It comes into operation somewhere between a population of 500,000 and 1 million. Under this size decline has few countervailing tendencies. Above this size the sheer size of the local market and the political and social importance of the city can generate some resistance to decline. Below, the ratchet and decline can lead to a free-fall; above, the rachet and decline can be ameliorated by the strength of the local urban economy and the weight of local political representation.

Small cities, a narrow reliance on manufacturing, remoteness from large metropolitan regions, a local economy dominated by big firms, and a lack of a tradition of entrepreneurship are some of the preconditions for job loss leading to economic decline. All cities in the Western world have experienced a measure of job loss. In the 1970s, for example, the city of Reading in England suffered a massive loss of traditional manufacturing. The traditional base of beer, bulbs, and biscuits was undercut by restructuring and closures. This job loss, however, did not lead to economic decline because of the growth of employment in producer services, and the expanding high-technology sector meant new jobs. The people who lost their jobs in the brewery and the biscuit factories were not the same people who became computer analysts, but the local economy remained buoyant. In slump cities, by contrast, job loss leads to economic decline because there are few sources of job creation.

Urban Competition and the Global Economy

During a recession there is increased competition for a declining pool of investment. The result: more intense competition among cities. As the recession deepens, the competition increases. In the global economy, the competition is not restricted to national boundaries. Seattle is not just competing with Portland or even Phoenix and Chicago for mobile capital; it has to compete with Hong Kong, Singapore, Kandy, Tijuana, and Bangkok. The net effect is to deflate wages and lower living standards. Of course Tijuana cannot compete with Seattle in aircraft manufacture. Not yet anyway. We can imagine a continuum of competitiveness from aircraft to transistor radios. Aircraft is still a high-technology, high-craft content process. It cannot be done just anywhere. Radios, in contrast, can be made anywhere. Aircraft will be made in Seattle but radios will be made in the cheapest place. As aircraft manufacture becomes more like radio manufacture (the end result of economic competition), aircraft will be made in the cheapest location, and jobs in aircraft manufacture will not pay as high as they do just now. In effect technological change in association with the globalization of the economy is leading to increased urban competition and a deflation of wages. Where this has proved more difficult, aircraft manufacture or business services, competition is less and cities with a spatial monopoly and the people who work there will maintain their higher living standards.

With the decline of national systems of regulation, local labor markets become a significant variable in explaining wage rates, conditions of employment, and work practices. The general effect is to make local labor markets, just as much as the national economy, an important backdrop in negotiations between capital and labor over wage rates and conditions of employment. The experience of similar groups of workers and hence particular types of households may vary by place. Where you live and work becomes an important determinant of standard of living and quality of life. As locality becomes an important determinant of relative bargaining power, differences occur as much by place as by economic sector or socioeconomic position. The same locality has

different communities and similar communities may have varying fortunes in different localities.

The experience of manufacturing employment may be a valuable pointer to the future. Let us summarize. In a period of
globalization of the capitalist economy and a regime of flexible
accumulation when manufacturing is no longer tied to traditional
urban economies, the urban order is subject to fundamental
change. Large cities such as New York and London experience
growing polarization of the workforce as traditional manufacturing jobs disappear, employment moves to the suburbs, and the
central city fractures along the deepening divides of race and
class. While new growth cities emerge, cities whose economy was
based on traditional manufacturing lose their economic raison
d'être and have to find new sources of investment and employment. Restructuring of the economy involves spatial reorganization of society.

New Images for Old Cities

The increasing competition between cities is felt in a variety of
ways. In this section I want to look at the generation of urban images. A recent advertisement for a Canon camera had the slogan
"Image Is Everything." Let us see how this slogan has been acted
upon in an era of intense competition, beginning at the very top
of the hierarchy.

At the level of the global urban hierarchy, we can identify
three world cities—London, New York, and Tokyo. They constitute a cross-section of the three most recent economic powers—
Britain of the nineteenth-century empire, the United States of the
twentieth century, and the emerging Japanese superpower. There
is both competition and collusion among these three. They compete for business and do business. They provide a temporal cov-

erage of incessant business. They need each other to provide a wide time coverage for international dealing in stocks, shares, bonds, futures, currency, and commodities. The stability and relative security of their position allow them the luxury of a *metropolitan provincialism*—a belief that the world is their city and a comforting sense that, if you stand in Covent Garden, Fifth Avenue, or the Marunouchi district, that world's most important business deals, cultural commentators, and social movements will pass through.

It is below this level that the greatest competition takes place. We can identify three groups:

- Wannabee World Cities.
- Clean and Green.
- Look, no more factories!

Wannabee World Cities

Wannabee world cities include Paris, Los Angeles, Chicago, Milan, Frankfurt, Melbourne, and Toronto.

A good though not infallible guide is to look at the cities that have applied to host the Olympic Games or have hosted the games in recent years. These include Seoul, Los Angeles, Atlanta, Barcelona, and Birmingham, England. To host the games is to achieve media coverage of a global spectacle; it implies that you need and want media coverage. It means you have world city pretensions if not quite there. The desire is prompted by the growth machine in individual cities—politicians, business leaders, developers, local elites, often in association with organized labor. The lure is status, income, development, wealth, and power. The drive for world-city status is prompted by the feeling that there are footloose business opportunities from conventions to corporate relocations—which can be attracted to successful cities. Get the right world-city image and the business will come.

Wannabee world cities are marked by a kind of nervous insecurity. They have an acute concern with their role and position in the global network of global cultural capital. Hence, the importance given to art galleries, big-name architects, academic schools, and art traditions. An edgy sense of not being at the center combines with a rather brittle cultural boosterism.

Clean and Green

In the advanced capitalist countries, the annihilation of space and time allows a more serious consideration of smaller towns and cities as places to do world and national business.

One important selling point for places with good accessibility is that they are not big cities like London or Paris or Atlanta. They are clean and green. Unpolluted. Closer to nature. The "old" image of such cities as Seattle and Portland or the emerging technology-based areas in Provence is of noncities. They have the advantages of cities without the disadvantages. The "purity" of these cities is not only their relationship with nature; it implies preurban, preindustrial. In the United States in particular, this implies places where there is no organized working class, strong regulatory bodies, or redistributional interventionist states. New definitions of purity are constantly introduced as clean and green cities become "developed."

Look, No More Factories!

There are a large number of cities in the advanced capitalist world whose economic growth and prosperity were based on manufacturing employment. Examples range from Pittsburgh to Glasgow, Syracuse to Scranton. The global shift of manufacturing has left these cities in need of a new economic base, a whole image. They are associated with the old as opposed to the new, the polluted in contrast with the clean, work in comparison with leisure. The phrase "look, no more factories" encapsulates their attempt to create a postindustrial image. This image involves a distancing from the industrial legacy, sometimes even a conscious distancing through the historicizing of industrial districts and the creation of factory museums and industrial heritage sites.

The physical reconstruction of parts of the city become crucial metaphors for the phoenixlike rise from the ashes of industrialism. Old harbor fronts turned into leisure, old industrial districts transformed into postmodern business parks. There is a powerful financial incentive to these land-use changes, but there is also an important symbolism—saddled with a negative industrial legacy, these cities seek to restructure their image. Even the terms *renewal, revitalization,* and *renaissance* all bespeak redemption through change.

Another important element in this transformation is the renegotiation of the contract with the physical environment. One of the most important legacies of their industrial past was a polluted and disfigured environment. Lakes and rivers that were previously considered dumping grounds now become central to a new discourse. Cleaning up pollution is not only a mandated responsibility; it becomes an act of redemption, the forging of a new contract, the reconstruction of a new place. The clean air of Pittsburgh becomes a peg on which to hang a whole range of transformative discourses. When a *National Geographic* reporter wrote about the city, "Pittsburgh's air is cleaner than ever, and its waters run clear," he was telling the tale of a born-again city (Miller 1991).

Cities compete for business, trade, and investment. They struggle for corporate attention. What sells the city is the image of the city. In a very real sense the city becomes the image. Business journals are full of urban images; the space economy involves the marketing of places. The images can be realistic, parodies, stereotypical. There are a number of different devices and marketing strategies. Here, I am concerned with the superimages that can be identified. These are the dominant images that are often superimposed one on another and cut across the different categories of cities. Four main images can be identified: fun city, green city, culture city, and pluralist city.

Fun City

Fun city is the conspicuous consumption of leisure—it is the beach, where only the beautiful can be seen. The city, like the predominance of body shots of attractive young women used in much of the advertising, is laid before the eager consumer eager to meet their needs, willing to satisfy their fantasies. It is a place where the sky is blue and where people smile and laugh. There are no problems to wrinkle the landscape or the lifestyle of the hyperfun city. Come to work in fun city, and it won't seem like work. Efficiency in the fun city does not imply the Protestant work ethic or deferred gratification.

Green City

Then there are the green cities, where a nature safely controlled and manicured provides a close though comforting experience with the semiwild while also providing room service and fax. As in the fun city, water is an important icon, along with fresh air, mountain vistas, and lack of traffic.

Culture City

After the beach, what? Here the emphasis is on a manicured and sanitized cultural experience from high-class shopping malls to symphony orchestras to art galleries. It involves the representation of the city as a cultural festival. Music festivals for the small cities, resident world-famous conductors for the bigger cities. The underlying message is to assure the discriminating that this is no hick town; this is a place of sophistication, well wired to the flow of global culture.

Pluralist City

The pluralist image is associated with the culture theme. Now the message is, come and experience the rich mix of different life-styles. It also links in with the pleasure theme: the urban experience is just one round of different ethnic holidays, constant fun-filled days with a never-ending cycle of festivities and celebrations.

This is the upside of multiculturalism: the pluralist dream of different ethnic groups adding to each other's experience but with no struggle over scarce resources or cultural identity, mixed but nice, varied but safe. It is the definition of multiculturalism as the blending of sushi bars with rap music and Armenian holidays. It is the reduction of cultural identity to modes of consumption.

These are difficult times for cities. The competition is now global, not just national or regional. In recession and downturns, the competition becomes even more severe. What becomes of crucial importance is for the city to identify its market niches and to construct the appropriate images for its market niches. The right combination of powerful images will not solve all the problems, but it sure does help. Maybe the Canon advertisement got it right.

The Postmodern City

Changes in advertising imagery are more for external consumption than internal use. Inside the city some of the most important changes have been described with the term *postmodern*. We need to take some care to understand the many implications of this word. As used here it implies a rupture with the past. I will concentrate on three aspects: the "new" look, the "new" enclosure movement, and the "new" civic culture.

The "New" Look

In the past twenty-five years the whole look of central cities has been changed. The straight-lined, flat-topped modernist towers now have to compete with buildings in a variety of shapes and colors, office blocks designed as Greek temples, and corporate offices built to look like Renaissance palaces. The modernist blocks look austere in comparison with this riot of color, shape, and ornamentation. Square buildings have been given new angles, flat roofs have been given pediments, glass walls now have holes in them or baroque-heavy detailing. We can understand this shift as one more round of architectural fashion. In the 1960s modernist architecture was all the rage, no self-respecting architect would be seen designing an office block with any ornamentation. By the 1990s a postmodern look was the fashion, and young architects looked down on all those straight lines. It is the fate of all new fashions to be seen as revolutionary, then standard, and then merely boring. In architecture, as in much of life, nothing dates so quickly as the most recent.

But there is something more than a shift in style. There is a deeper message to be drawn than the fickleness of design. The shift from modern to postmodern, which we can date around the early 1970s, came at a time of increasing competition between cities. When a sharp cleavage occurs as in the modern/postmodern shift, buildings and cities can look very dated very quickly. The building boom of the 1980s gave an added opportunity for the new look. The postmodern shift was part of an attempt at differentiation between cities at a time of growing global competition. There was a surge of both new building and refurbishment, all in the new styles in an attempt to seem still connected to the global culture of capital. As cities chased after mobile capital they wanted to present a contemporary view, an image of being on the cutting edge. The postmodern look gave that image. Behind the shift in style was an attempt not to be caught in the past. The need to appear contemporary arose from the need to attract and retain mobile capital. The look of cities became an important cause and effect of interurban competition. The competition of the present helps explain the dive into the architectural past.

The "New" Enclosure Movement

The postmodern city is more than just a collection of new buildings. There is a new syntax as well as new words to this architectural shift. There is what I will refer to as the "new" enclosure movement. The first enclosures occurred in England, reaching their peak in the last half of the eighteenth and first part of the nineteenth centuries. Enclosures meant the privatizing of open common lands and involved the enclosing of open fields and the private appropriation of public pastures. The modern enclosure occurs in urban areas and can be seen in many different ways. There has been the creation of what we may rightly call bunker architecture. More and more buildings seek to regulate access. More than this they seek to hide access. The blank wall is a withdrawal from a civic culture. For example, more and more hotels in downtown locations seek to hide their entrances, block their entrances, or restrict them to the ordinary citizen. Walls come down to the street, entrances are taken away from direct street level, and access has to be negotiated. The result is the closing off from public space. There has also been the rise of "gated" communities. These are communities that have gates to keep out all but the residents and their friends. Private security guards, walls, gates, and electric fences all reflect a concern with safety and a palpable expression of fear of the urban "other." The gates reinforce the misgivings we have of one another. The shared space of the city becomes the segmented segregation of tiny communities fearful of the rest of the city. There is a shattering of the notion of a collective good into the kaleidoscope of individual anxieties. Our cities now reflect our sense of apprehension more than our sense of hope. In his book on Los Angeles, Mike Davis has a chapter on Fortress L. A.; some of the section headings tell us much about the contemporary enclosure movement: "The Destruction of Public Space," "The Forbidden City," "Sadistic Street Environments," "Frank Gehry as Dirty Harry," "The Panoptican Mall," "From Rentacop to Robocop," "The Fear of Crowds" (Davis 1990). In varying degrees these headings would serve for books about other cities around the world.

The "New" Civic Culture

The new look of cities reflects and embodies a "new" civic culture. This new culture has emerged at a time of increasing competition at the global, national, and urban levels. When combined with a recession, the result is a fiscal crisis that is interpreted as the need to curtail social expenditures. The consequence, around the world, is a decline in the benevolence of national and urban governments toward welfare, public goods, and many of those things that add to the quality of urban life. Public transport has been cut back, spending on cultural affairs and environmental quality lowered, and the creation and maintenance of urban public spaces reduced. There are exceptions. French cities, Paris in particular, have emerged as a major exception to this trend. And the base point obviously varies around the world. Swedish and Dutch cities, for example, still have an incomparably higher level of public expenditure than cities in the United States.

In the "new" civic culture, more emphasis has been placed on revenue-generating rather than revenue-disposing. The needs of business have been returned to a dominating primacy, and footloose capital has been wooed with all manner of incentives, grants, and tax breaks. As recession deepens the bidding intensifies as cities compete one with another. City governments have also taken a more active role in land development deals and in the encouragement of revenue-generating activities. The redistributional city is turning into the entrepreneurial city.

There are countervailing tendencies. In the cities of the rich countries, many people are just as concerned with the quality of employment as the quantity of employment. In the 1990s, as before, those who are struggling will perhaps take any job; but more and more people are concerned with finding employment that not only pays well but is socially useful and ecologically respectful and provides enough slack to allow time to enjoy the nonworking hours. As economic growth and income maximization have to compete as social and personal goals with ecological responsibility and maximization of the quality of life, the nature of citizen activity will change. People will become even more concerned with the quality of public services; and after the private greed of the 1980s, public responsibility will become an important social objective. The fundamental question is, can the rhetoric be turned into reality? That will be the battle for citizen activists of the future.

In the poorer cities of the world most citizens do not yet have the luxury of choice. For many the basic necessities are still the main goal in life. But we would do well to look at the struggles and successes of Third World citizens with more than just patronizing interest. For too long the question has been, how can we export techniques and technology from the rich world to the poor world? The results have been ludicrous—motorways built for cities where most people are too poor to afford private cars—if not downright dangerous—telling mothers to feed their children (inferior) powdered milk rather than (the more nutritious) breast milk. A more radical solution is to look at the self-help strategies and low-tech solutions used by citizens of many Third World cities and to see them as prototypes for more universal application. This is not to romanticize Third World poverty but to suggest that we can learn something from the success stories of people in poorer cities who have realized that ultimately the most important resource of any city is its citizens.

The "new" civic culture of the 1990s and beyond will be a curious mixture of the return to a domination by business interests and the evolution of a new enlightened public interest. The "welfare" state, at least in its most expansive phase, will be seen as a thing of the past, a curious time when rising real incomes and sustained economic growth allowed a social contract based on the need and ability to create domestic harmony. But the demise of the old welfare state will not imply a return to the prewelfare state. There are too many articulate and powerful people who rely on the range of public services. A new set of business ethics will also be forged just as a new fiscal agenda for the public sector is being created. The new civic culture will be a combination of the imperatives of business, ecological responsibility, and a concern with the quality of life. They will increasingly be seen as interrelated rather than separate considerations. A city with a healthy environment and a good quality of life will be more likely to attract and retain business. The more enlightened business will see the economic sense of spending money on environmental cleanup and good education. There will be variations. The richer cities are likely to get richer, and those left out of the benign cycle of growth and investment may languish. And the patterns of investment will, as usual, pay more heed to the rich and the powerful than to the poor and needy. The "new" of the emerging civic culture, however, does at least allow an opportunity for debate and criticism. When things are in flux as we approach the second millenium, as in the reorganization of the new world order and new urban order, alternative voices have a greater opportunity to be heard. For a new world, we need a new rhetoric.

Part Two

New Geographies

4

On Being an Academic

We can conceptualize the world as three separate but interrelated dimensions: the global economy, national societies, and local communities. We all live in a variety of communities, some more local than others. I first write these lines as I look out onto my garden in the small upstate New York village of Cazenovia. I coach soccer here, ski with friends on Friday nights in the winter, drink in the local tavern. I am also connected by technology (television, radio, and various computer networks) to people who share my interests yet live all over the country and all around the globe. I also belong to an extended family centered around the small Scottish village of Tullibody but connected all over the world. And then there are my professional connections. I teach in a geography department, a small community within the larger community of a university. In all of these different communities I have varied and different roles. I am neighbor and resident, uncle and brother, teacher and advisor, colleague and academic. In this chapter I want to consider the professional community in which I make a living, find an identity, and conduct my work.

Early Years

My paternal grandmother had eleven children. None of them went to university. Up until the 1960s, it was expensive and restricted to the wealthy and to a few token poor people. Universities in Britain were elitist institutions, finishing schools for the ruling class.

By the time my generation was in high school, things had begun to change. Compared to the United States, the change was still snail-paced slow. There was still selection at age eleven for grammar school, with the vast majority programmed to fail and shunted off to the more vocational training of secondary modern schools; universities were still dominated by the products of fee-paying schools, and the whole educational system was devised to fail most students so that a tiny minority could be weeded out. The emphasis was on failing as many people as possible in order to reward the tiny minority who succeeded.

I, along with some of my cousins, went to university. We were all helped by supportive families who were eager for their children to do well. There was an ambiguity. The parents wanted their children to gain as high an academic success as possible. Education was the way to get good, high-paying, secure jobs. With qualifications you did not have to work in the coal mines or serve people in a shop. The ideal was to become a schoolteacher—a white-collar job, secure pay, and long summer holidays. What more could you ask for? But there was also a tinge of anxiety behind the encouragement. Jealousy that the children were able to do things denied to them. Fear that educational attainment would take the children into realms where the parents had no knowledge, no authority, no power. The unspoken dread that the children would learn to despise their own parents and deny their background for middle-class respectability.

We were also helped by an impressive public education system. Most of us went to Alloa Academy, the county grammar school well endowed with gifted teachers. I went there in 1963. These were good years. It was a time when people were becoming more affluent, more confident. Education was well funded by the Local Councils, particularly in Scotland, where there was a strong emphasis on education, the roots of which lie in the Calvinist tradition. This religious doctrine, which promoted an individual dialogue with God as opposed to the Catholic notion of a collective mediation through a hierarchical priesthood, had to stress reading and writing skills for believers to be able to read the Bible. From this theological position grew an increasingly secular commitment to a more open, well-funded education system.

I was part of a lucky cohort. My educational attainments were not so much the result of individual effort but of a collective commitment by both my family and the local society to improve education. When I went to the grammar school along with one of my cousins, there were already three other cousins. I did not face the agonizing loneliness of the isolated scholarship student who figures so largely in British intellectual life. I was surrounded by friends and family.

The expectation at my grammar school was that you were going to university. The expectation was so much a part of the fabric of the school that it was easy to fulfill. In 1969 I went to Aberdeen University. I, like almost every other British university student at that time, was given a grant from the government to pay the fees and provide living expenses. I went initially to study English literature. But in the Scottish university system, then a four-year course, you also had to take other courses. I took geology because I needed a science subject and geography because I had got high grades at school.

The system stressed individual responsibility. You went to

lectures if you wanted. There was no one to tell you to work. I enjoyed the freedom. Most of the lecturers were good, a tiny minority were inspiring, with only a small percentage bordering on the incompetent. The real education of universities was outside the books and the lectures; it was in meeting new people, doing different things, trying on new identities. I read a lot, experimented with lots of things, reveled in my freedom, and, most of all, talked and talked with friends and fellow students as we sought to discover the world and to find ourselves. It was a great time. I have of course forgotten all the bad times. Memory is selective; and the further I am from the experience, the more my memory filters out the sad times. But I must have enjoyed it at the time, as well as in the act of memory, because, when I was close to graduating, I wanted to continue the experience. I did not feel ready to take up a career, fill a slot in a corporate hierarchy, or settle down to suburban domesticity. I applied to various universities to do graduate work. I was rejected by some but accepted at Bristol.

Graduate School

I went to Bristol University in 1973. I had been given a grant from the Social Science Research Council. The public funding of my private journey continued. We too often imagine our accomplishments to be the product of individual effort. My own efforts were important, but I also realize that there was another side. My journey was made easier by government spending. I received a grant to go to university as both an undergraduate and a postgraduate. The grant was not huge, I had little left over after basic needs were met, but I could live and concentrate on my work without having to borrow too much money or take an outside job. I was very fortunate to pursue my education at a time of relatively generous government funding.

To be a graduate student in 1973 in a good geography department was to be in an exciting environment. There were a lot of graduate students, rare at the time in British universities, and a healthy debate. The quantitative revolution in British geography had one of its major centers in Bristol. And there were the first stirrings of a Marxist critique. I had the feeling of being on the cusp of intellectual change and discovery. I did not realize how lucky I was until I experienced other graduate schools with all their cliques and factions and bitter infighting. At Bristol it either did not exist much, or else I was blissfully unaware of its existence. I had time to think and read and write. I was encouraged and nurtured.

I enjoyed it so much that when I finished I wanted to continue the experience. I was given a postdoctoral fellowship to work on inner-city housing markets. This was even better than being a graduate student. I was doing research but now being paid a salary. My outgoings were tiny in relation to my income. In terms of disposable income, it was one the richest periods in my life. It was also one of the most intellectually fascinating. I had few teaching or administrative responsibilities; and the person I worked with, Keith Bassett, was a great friend as well as a stimulating colleague. We climbed mountains in north Wales and the Alps, played squash and tennis, drank in pubs, did research on the inner city, and sought to understand what a Marxist geography could look like. It was a great time.

My fellowship was for only two years. I had been applying for jobs but without much success. Then in 1978 I was offered a lectureship at Reading University. My academic career had begun.

I have taught at universities in Britain, Europe, Australia, and the United States. I have given invited lectures and been to many national and international conferences. I have, in short, been around the academic community for some time. Before making some general observations that are firmly rooted in these experiences, let me say something about my particular perspective.

On Being an Academic Geographer

It begins generally with the statement, "That's interesting. It was my favorite subject at school." The word *favorite* can be substituted by *best/worst/easiest/hardest/* or any one of a number of different adjectives.

To the outside world to be an academic is the source of some interest but to be an academic geographer is the source of some bemusement. "You mean you study that at university?" "But don't we know where everywhere is now?"

Geography lacks the arcane sense of mystery that physics, mathematics, or chemistry has, the career mission of law and engineering, or the seemingly applied dimension of economics and political science. It sounds too easy to generate great respect and too common to invoke great wonder. If the academy is like the global economy, then geography is a poor Third World country.

As a subject geography has a long history; but as a formal academic discipline, it owes a great deal to the imperial mission of the late nineteenth century. It is no accident that geography is particularly strong in Britain, where it grew as an "aid to statecraft," in the words of the geographer Sir Halford John Mackinder (1861–1947). Since then it has prospered and has also had some setbacks. It is firmly entrenched in the major universities of Britain, Canada, Australia, and most of Europe, although many of the "new" universities of the 1960s and 1970s did not have geography. In the United States, the position is more precarious, with no geography departments in the most prestigious universities of Harvard, Princeton, Yale, Stanford, and Chicago. Although there are many strong geography programs in the United States, the discipline as a whole is on the margins of academic numbers, power, and prestige. This is both a cause and effect of the lack of self-confidence in the discipline.

The great strength and great weakness of academic geography is its lack of a coherent center. Geography does not have the firm center of neoclassical economics, the studied concern on the "native other" of anthropology, or the corpus of great classics of sociology. There are few generally agreed-upon classics; and rather than a firm center, there is a series of fluctuating, overlapping peripheries. There are as many geographies as there are geographers. But this anarchy is also a source of strength. It makes geography one of the most vibrant subjects, like many Third World countries, the scene of continual revolution and counterrevolution. Compared to geography most of the other social sciences are staid and boring. It is the difference between Switzerland and Latin America. The Third World metaphor is illuminating. Like a poor country, geography "imports" most of its theories. There is a whole faction of comprador intellectuals in geography who make their reputation by importing the most recent theories; and like the sellers of foreign cars and videos, they make high profit if they can control the distribution. The export countries vary over time. In the 1960s it was the natural sciences, in the 1970s political economy, and by the late 1980s and early 1990s, it was the humanities supplying the dominant fashions. Geographers lack the self-confidence to do much value-added work. Geography exports raw materials but imports the theory from elsewhere. The relationship between geography and the dominant exporter varies between that of Mexico and the United States, and that of Canada and the United States. In the free-trade zone of the academy, geography has a position of inferiority.

I am more than just a geographer. The disciplinary label is

important but only partly revealing. I am white, male, British, but living in the United States. All of these give color, substance, and direction to my view of the world. I am also at a particular stage in my career. In 1987–88 I wrote a paper that was published in an academic journal in 1989. I thought it was a good paper. The next issue of the journal contained an article devoted entirely to criticizing my paper. I was flattered. I was stung. But what really got to me was a realization. As I read the critical response, I recalled a paper that I had written in 1976; they both had the same ring of arrogant self-confidence, aggressive criticism, and desire to carve out a name. First time round it was me doing the criticizing, second time I was the object of criticism. I seemed to have moved from bright young thing to boring old fart. I felt like one of those car advertisements, from 0 to 60 in ten seconds. In my case it was from graduate student to professor in the blink of an eye. Outsider to insider, periphery to core, revolutionary to establishment. Change does not so much creep up on us; sometimes, we are walking along and it just comes up and mugs us in broad daylight.

Academic Life

For me academic life is one of the most satisfying as well as the most frustrating of experiences. Satisfying to the extent that I am given the privilege of being paid for something I love doing. For me researching, writing, and teaching are not a job but a pleasure. Sometimes I still cannot believe that I get paid for doing it. I moan about my teaching load or how much writing I have got to do, but these complaints are part of the way we negotiate with other people or pass messages to each other about how hard we are working.

The frustrations are to do with the ambiguities involved in

the individual/collective nature of the academic enterprise. Let me look at three: discipline and punishment, the war of the paper clips, and the ivory tower.

Discipline and Punishment

Academic subjects are sometimes referred to as a discipline. A strange little word, full of hidden meanings and unexploded implications of linguistic ambiguity. Turn to a dictionary. In mine, under *discipline*, are the words

> instruction: training or mode of life in accordance with rules: subjection to control: order: severe training: mortification: punishment: an instrument of penance or punishment.

Punishment seems to go along with discipline. From the outside it seems an unusual combination. Not for those in the community. Let me elaborate with an anecdote. In 1980 I had my first book published. The book, entitled *Housing and Residential Structure*, was co-written with my friend and colleague Keith Bassett. It was a good book that surveyed the literature in the field and codified a Marxist perspective on cities and housing production and consumption. Several years later I submitted a paper to an academic journal. The editor, as is usual practice, sent my paper out to anonymous reviewers. The editor sent me the reviews. One reviewer wrote, "This paper fails to draw attention to the work of Bassett and Short." When I got the review, I wanted to shout out, "But I am the Short of Bassett and Short. The very same. How could I not draw attention to the work of Bassett and Short? I am he. One half of the combination. It was I who wrote some of that book!"

It begins early. As an undergraduate you have to read other people's work. You are graded by how much you know of other people's work. As a graduate student, you are socialized into a culture that, at its worst, minimizes your individual contribution. Your job is to read certain authors and write in a certain way. Not the flights of fancy of the creative writing program, nor the punchy style of journalist courses. No. For the academic graduate student the writing has to detail what other people write and be in a style that, if marketed by an aggressive drug company, would be the biggest-selling sleeping pill. There is a point to it. It avoids the reinvention of the wheel, it gives due recognition to other people's contributions, and the writing style is meant to be clear and "objective." That is its best. All too often it degenerates into a mindless repetition of citations, an intellectual paralysis that avoids creative thought, and is all wrapped in a style that would be anemic if it were alive.

Behind the liberalism of contemporary intellectual practice lies a very narrow definition of what academic work is and how academics should write. The orthodoxy is maintained by advisors of graduate students, who teach them that there is a "proper" way for academics to write and a "proper" way of doing research. In my experience, this narrowing of student talents is most marked in US universities, which have a more professional attitude to graduate studies. Along with professionalism comes orthodoxy. The orthodoxy is maintained throughout an academic's career. The currency of academic life is publication. But to publish an academic must brave the reviewing process. To get a book published or an article accepted in an academic journal your work is assessed by other people. Manuscripts and papers are sent out to anonymous reviewers. Their job is to make comments, pass judgments. At its best the reviewing process is a form of quality control. And it can improve the quality of work. I have received comments from journal reviewers that have pointed to weaknesses and suggested improvements to my early drafts. This is the process working well. At its worst it creates an orthodoxy that leads to the mortification of the living by the dead and the domination of the present by the past.

To be an academic is to be part of a collective enterprise with rites, rules, and standards. To be an academic author is both to reinforce and to challenge the collective. Writing maintains the academy; but individual authors have to be disciplined, not allowed to get too far out-of-bounds—they have to be kept in check. In Australia there is something called the "tall poppy syndrome." Poppies that get too tall are cut down. And in Japan there is a widely used expression that means, roughly translated, "the nail that stands up is hammered down." In the academy, with its system of anonymous reviewing and continual scrutiny and criticism, there are many opportunities to cut down the tall poppy, hammer down the nail. Reviews and criticisms are a form of damage-limitation control with no single author being allowed to undermine the collective. Exceptions are made if the author is very dead or very foreign. Being alive and not foreign is not good for your academic reputation. To be an academic author is to subject yourself to constant criticism, continual scrutiny. The great Australian painter Sir Sydney Nolan was once asked how he responded to criticism. "Survive the punishment" was his advice. Good advice for the potential academic.

To be part of an academic discipline is to take part in an exciting adventure, but it also is to be part of an exercise in social control, personal mortification, and intellectual punishment. Maybe the dictionary entry was not so far off the mark.

The War of the Paper Clips

Jung identified four different types of personality based on their predominant response to the world; these were sensation, thinking, feeling, and intuition types. The academic world is dominated by thinking types. Jung is too obtuse a writer to quote with much effect, so let me instead quote from one of the clearest Jungian interpreters, Frieda Fordham. Modern readers may be offended by the sexist bias of the language, but stick with it:

> When the life of an individual is mainly ruled by thinking and his actions are usually the result of an intellectually considered motive, he may be fairly called a thinking type. This type "thinks things out" and comes to conclusions based on objective data—what he calls facts. He likes logic and order, and is fond of inventing neat formulae to express his views. He bases his life on principles and would like to see others do the same (Fordham 1966, 37).

Jung also wrote about the shadow. This is the dark side of the unconscious. You always know the shape of your shadow by the people you dislike the most; you dislike them because they represent qualities that you have yet to disown. For the thinking types, the shadow contains emotions and feeling. Fordham continues with her description of the thinking type:

> He believes that he is rational and logical, but in fact he suppresses all that does not fit into his scheme, or refuses to recognize it. . . . he represses emotion and feeling. . . . he suffers from irrational moods which he does not admit (ibid).

The thinking type is just that, a representative type. It is a tendency, an archetype rather than a description of an actual person. But the generalization contains the seeds of an important truth about academic life.

It was Henry Kissinger who said that academic battles are so vindictive because the stakes are so low. Another reason is that below all that cool rationality and icy logic there is a rich stew of bubbling emotion that is all the more potent because it is so unexamined, unrecorded, and ignored. How else to explain the sheer nastiness of academic disputes? People get upset over what seem like trivial things; the title of this section is not accidental. Academics do fall out over such things as the use or nonuse of paper clips in departmental papers. I am not immune from this kind of thing. This is not the report of a dispassionate observer. I mix it up as well as anyone. But what always surprises me is the depth of emotion at even the quietest faculty meetings. The suppression of emotion in the private work of the thinking type is given extraordinary vent in the public discussion. Faculty meetings can be more vindictive than the bloodiest of religious differences, academic disputes have a virulence bordering on religious wars, and animosity between individual academics is played out with the same conviction as the battle for papal succession in Renaissance Italy. That the cause of the disputes and their wider social consequences are so minor seems not so much beside the point as the point, as if their very irrelevancy simply fueled the anxiety and rancor. Academic life gives proof positive to Schopenhauer's thesis that intelligence is nothing more than a servant of blind will.

Academic socialization encourages such behavior. Academics become academics because they have scholastic aptitude. They are academically bright, good at school, with impressive grades. Their parents are often proud of them. They go to university and then graduate school. The academy even has as its folk hero the absent-minded professor who knows complicated formulae but cannot remember where the bathroom is. There is even a cult of eccentricity. Now it is more surface than substance, as if forgetting where the bathroom is makes up for having an undistinguished academic career. Oxbridge is full of rather pathetic characters who generate minor eccentricities as a desperate attempt at individuality. There is the US equivalent, the so-called tweed belt from Boston, through Chicago, and into Berkeley, Palo Alto; and Westwood in Los Angeles has its fair share of fake Oxbridge dons replete with pipe, jackets with leather patches at the elbow, and contempt for US popular culture.

People skills are accidental to the academic pursuit. In all the academic training, minds not hearts are developed. There are some wonderfully warm academics; but as a group, as a collective enterprise they lack heart, soul, and compassion. And it is all the sadder because when there is emotion it is often a torrent of uncontrolled bile and venom. Academic instruction can too often be like the revenge of the nerds, the bright insecure kids getting back at the more popular, but less academically gifted kids.

Rugged individualism has a huge role to play in academic life. To follow a long, lonely path that is out of step with the quick-investment, quick-return mentality of the present era, to work at something over the years in a field that is neither lucrative, popular, nor fashionable requires a strong sense of individual presence. To do really good work you have to stand out, to be out of step. The strong individuality of the contemporary academic can embody these attractive traits, but all too often it can also reflect a mind unconnected to the heart, unclaimed feelings, and a social inadequacy rather than a truly creative mind.

The life of the mind is a noble, enlightening enterprise that can cast great light on the workings of the world. But like all bright flames, it casts a giant shadow.

The Ivory Tower

A common complaint is that universities in general and academics in particular are not connected enough with the rest of life.

The term *ivory tower* is used as a criticism. My own feelings in this matter are more complex; universities are both too much of an ivory tower and too little of an ivory tower. Let me explore this paradox.

Many of the earliest universities were religious institutions. The term *chair*, for example, comes from Arabic and the practice of wise men dispensing wisdom around the mosque while sitting in a big chair. In medieval Europe the early universities were separated out from the rest of society. The teachers were members of religious orders and thus subject to different rules of behavior, different codes of conduct. They were in principle, if rarely in practice, supposed to renounce earthly pleasures, live up to vows of celibacy and poverty, and leave behind them ties of family and kinship. It is this separation that fueled the notion and the practice of universities as disconnected from everyday life. Even up to the early twentieth century, Oxford dons in certain colleges had to renounce their fellowships on getting married. Such things allowed the image of universities as ivory towers to persist. Today, people who teach at universities have the same basic issues as other people to contend with—how to make a living, raise a family, make a reputation, pursue relationships, find happiness. People in contemporary universities are not so different from the rest of the population. Much has been made of the easy life of academics. In the 1980s in the United States, there was a spate of books on the underworked, overpaid professoriat. These books prove my point. Academics are now subject to the same criteria as people in other occupations. The books, in their different ways, reinforce this idea by pointing to the putative difference between the myth and the reality. Academics, the authors argue, should be judged along with everyone else. There is no longer any religious justification to a separate academic sphere.

But universities are an ivory tower. Not in the sense that academics have an easier life than anyone else. There are some work-shy individuals and some who take the money and run, but not any more or any less than in most occupations and professions. Neither goodness nor villainy is a monopoly of the campus. The ivory tower I refer to is the hermetic nature of much of the academic discussions. There is a self-referential quality to the debates in the humanities and social sciences that can too often miss a connection with the rest of society. Take academic publications. Academics make their reputations by publishing books and articles. Some are meant to be read. Most are just meant to be published. Academic journals are bought by libraries. Some are read, others are not. To get published you have to subscribe to the tenets of the journal. There are now enough journals in any one field to provide an avenue for the least impressive papers. Disciplines acknowledge this fact by having a core set of journals that are considered of higher quality. The periphery is large and has a big demand for articles. And so we have academics wanting and needing to publish, journals wanting to publish, and libraries picking up the tab. Neither market forces nor consumer demand have much of a role. Now, some will argue that they have no place in academic matters, but what that leaves is a self-referential system open to abuse. In this, as in other ways, universities have become disconnected from a wider world.

The severing of contact between the universities and the wider public is also related to the changing role of intellectuals. The Italian Marxist Antonio Gramsci (1891–1937) identified a key role for intellectuals: they express the ideological struggle for political, economic, and cultural hegemony. The contemporary intellectuals are journalists, TV talk-show hosts, actors, and sports people. Academics have a role to play, and some play a major role; but compared to the great potential they contain, universities have abandoned a pivotal role as the setting for public intellectuals. Universities have been sidelined by technological and cultural changes, especially the importance of mass media in informing ideas. The peripheralization has also been accepted by many academics who prefer the safety and security of academic infighting to the bigger world of public debate and political controversy.

Many academics are wary of overtly public connections. Not because they want a quiet life. The demand for public relevance is mostly made by the rich and the powerful, and some academics are rightly wary of providing information and legitimation to the corporate elite. There is a culture of resistance in universities that needs to be maintained and fostered. Universities have a marvelous opportunity to provide a center of resistance to the crasser elements of contemporary society without losing sight of their public role. Universities have tremendous resources. They can give a sense of distance from the hurly-burly of the very contemporary without drifting off into the irrelevance of outer academic space. They have the possibility of offering a place of connection yet a necessary distance. Academics have an important role to play as intellectuals in the Gramscian sense of the word. There is the danger of the project being sabotaged by an inward spiral of self-referential navel gazing and too close an outer connection with only the very powerful, but there is an important space for academics to occupy between hermetic irrelevance and corporate sellout.

A Typology of Academics

So far I have been using the term *academic* to describe people who teach in the academy. At best the term is a blunt instrument. Anyone who has spent more than five minutes in a university will know that the term covers a range of very different people. Academics come in all shapes, sizes, opinions, and attitudes. Let me end this chapter with a slightly finer distinction. On the basis of my experience I can identify three different types: academics, scholars, and intellectuals.

Academics

They are concerned with the practice of being an academic. They have a greater involvement with the life of the academy. They would not miss a department or faculty meeting; they study the rule books; the smooth running of the place is one of their principal concerns. These are the people who are glad to give up the scholarly activity in order to do more administration. A strange paradox here. Few honestly admit this. They are continually saying how desperate they are to get down to some "real" work, but they know and everyone around them knows that what they really love is administration. Not for some more glorious end but for the order, the discipline, the organization. The best of them take their administrative job seriously, and they provide the necessary context for other activity to take place. As they get older, they end up being full-time administrators. Their career path is chairperson, dean and, for the most ambitious, chancellor, president, or whatever the name is given to the head honcho in the academic institution. The best of them are vital to the life of any academic enterprise. The worst of them hide their personal inadequacies behind a power relationship. For them power is not a means to an end but the end itself. To be sure the power is small, but for small people even a small amount of power is important.

Scholars

These are the people who devote more time and effort to doing research. At their best, they do work of originality and brilliance. Alas, this is all too rare. What often passes for scholarship is a very tight demarcation around a constricted subject in order for the researcher to attain some level of expertise and hence power by being considered an expert, asked to review book proposals, and referee academic papers. Scholars are most visible immediately after graduate school because academic publications are of major significance in getting a job, getting tenure, and being made a full professor. Scholars can and do become academics or intellectuals.

A distinction could be drawn between scholarship and publication. What is published in academic journals may not be scholarly, and some of the best scholarly work is very often not published as academic books or journals. There are now enough journals for almost any academic to find a fruitful source of publication. The appraisal of scholarly work is not easy and is definitely not unconnected to power, prestige, and influence. There is the well-known "halo" effect. Identical papers sent to journals are not reviewed in similar ways. Authors from prestige universities get more favorable treatment. Book reviewers and journal editors may treat powerful figures more leniently than they would some obscure figure with no power. These are facts of life in academe, as they are in all walks of life.

Intellectuals

The smallest group. They are concerned with their role in the wider community and use their scholarship and writing talents to connect with a wider public. Here is where Short's Law of Academic Envy comes into operation. The law states: the more successful intellectuals become, the more they are derided by the scholars and academics. John Kenneth Galbraith in economics, Carl Sagan in science, Paul Ehrlich in ecology. These are the people who the interested layperson reads and listens to with some care. Although different people with different interests, they all share the same fate: as successful intellectuals they are feared, despised, and distrusted by most of their professional colleagues. Intellectuals often start off as scholars. A typical biography would be a graduate student, a career scholar following the usual track, and then for a variety of reasons a shift into the wider realm of more public intellectual. Some of the reasons include the desire for money, boredom with early academic success, the need to communicate, a well-developed ego and sensitive social conscience. The reasons differ, but these people all have the courage to step out of the narrow mold of scholars. To write for a more general audience, their work has to be clear and accessible. But for some scholars, this open style is to let the public see behind the mystique of academic scholarship. Intellectuals make it seem easier than scholars consider necessary. The scholars may have a point. Intellectuals can be used by the media, governments, corporations, and interest groups of all sorts. In popularizing work intellectuals can get it wrong, they can play down the often important qualifiers for the sake of a glib remark, a epigrammatic explanation, a concise sound bite.

There is a connection between the three types. Most people have elements of all three types in their makeup. They can and do exist in the one person. People who work in universities have to attend meetings as well as write papers and communicate with a wider audience.

There is also an undeclared war between these different groups. The academics get paid more money, have the best parking, and don't do as much teaching. The more successful they become as academics, the less teaching and research they need to do. The scholars and intellectuals hate them because they have local power. It is the academics who allocate scarce resources and wield the hatchet that can draw blood. The academics, in turn, think they do all the necessary trench work that is absolutely vital but rarely given any recognition. The money and the parking are a small recompense for continual attendance at mind-numbing, boring meetings. Only they, the academics, have the overall vision of the department/school/university. They have to make difficult decisions and no-win choices about money and resources. They have to live in the real world.

The intellectuals and the academics think that the scholars are wackos, lost in a cozy, safe world, inattentive to wider concerns or pressing issues to the institution and to society. To be a scholar in your twenties and thirties is a sign of mature judgment; to be one in your forties and fifties is a sign of anal retentiveness. The academics get back at them by paying them less money and allotting them the parking spaces furthest from their offices.

The academics and the scholars distrust the intellectuals. They are envious of the successful ones, especially those who get their picture in the paper, have been seen on television, have lucrative book contracts, and are always cited by the mass media. If the intellectuals also happen to be personable and contented and with attractive spouses, the envy of the other two groups is barely concealed. There is no more virulent strain of ill-feeling than academic envy. The scholars continually bad-mouth the intellectuals and refuse them entry into their clubs or nominations for scholarly awards. The intellectuals, in turn, especially the successful ones, look down on the academics and the scholars. They feel one group spends too much time in committees and the other too much time in the archives or in the laboratory. The intellectuals feel misrepresented by the scholars and underpaid by the academics.

These three types constitute the context of my working life in the academy. It is aggravating and inspiring, happy and sad, uplifting and depressing, full of hope and rancor, supportive and critical, encouraging and depressing. It is from here that I see the world, understand the world, and live my working life.

5

Progressive Human Geography

The word *progress* has a curiously modern ring; it echoes all those discredited enlightenment projects. Its position in a book where postmodernism is counterposed to modernism may seem strange. It is strange. Despite all my exposure to postmodern writing and thought I cannot seem to throw off the idea that as a citizen and an academic I should be using my position in society and job skills to advance an emancipatory project. The task is beset with dangers of specification and intent. But for me it cannot be avoided.

We can distinguish between several types of progress. Publishing papers and books can help individuals progress up the career hierarchy. Progress in this way is a form of individual achievement. This is the *progress of geographers* and is evident in the array of citation indices continually referenced, cross-referenced, and rereferenced as well as in the attention given to "length" and "width" of publications and curriculum vitae in reviews of geography departments by funding bodies, and in individual staff-appraisal exercises. There is also the ability of specific disciplines to maintain or strengthen their position in the higher education sector. This is the *progress of geography*.

There is also *progress in geography*. This is often defined as the ability of geographers to make their world more understandable. Like all social projects, there are problems of definition. What do we mean by more knowledge? More understandable? There is also a deeper question of who decides what is progress? Academics live in a public world where businesses and governments have an important and powerful job in setting the research agenda, sometimes in broad general terms, other times in more specific ways.

Progress in human geography, I want to suggest, is not devoid of social implications or political consequences. The search for knowledge, even what constitutes knowledge, is a political act. There is no such thing as politically neutral or value-free research. In our institutionalized role as teachers and researchers, we are politically and socially implicated. Implicated but not necessarily compromised.

An important element in the history of geography has been the concern to engage with the outside world. Many have been eager to use their labor, knowledge, and techniques for a broader public purpose. The enterprise holds out the prospect of tremendous possibilities but is also beset with major problems. In his essay "The Function of the University in a Time of Crisis," Noam Chomsky points to some of the problems:

> Consider the often-voiced demand that the University serve the needs of the outside society—that its activities be "relevant" to general social concerns. Put in this way this demand is justifiable. Translated into practice, however, it usually means that

the universities provide a service to *existing* social institutions, those institutions that are in a position to articulate their needs and subsidize the effort to meet them. It is not difficult for members of the university community to delude themselves into believing that they are maintaining a "neutral value-free" position when they are simply responding to demands set elsewhere. In fact to do so is a political decision, namely to ratify the existing distribution of power, authority and privilege in the society at large and to take on a commitment to reinforce it. The Pentagon and the great corporations can formulate their needs and subsidize the kind of work that will answer to them. The peasants in Guatemala or the unemployed in Harlem are in no position to do so (Chomsky 1973, 89–90).

Chomsky's remarks are very pertinent at the moment, as geography seems bewitched by the notion of technical know-how, in particular geographical information systems (GIS). It is not, I believe, solely for intellectual or moral reasons but for the sake of political and fiscal expediency. GIS has enough buzzwords to attract funding from corporate interests eager to exploit new markets and government bodies keen to amass, order, and analyze data. Hardly a job advertisement appeared in the 1980s and early 1990s without a totemic reference to GIS. There *is* a need for GIS, but we need to ask whose geography? Whose information? Whose system? We know geography may get funding. But at what cost? We cannot read off public interest from the articulated concerns of major private and public institutions. When it is bereft of theory and devoid of moral purpose, GIS will degenerate into a shabby exercise in fashion following and a grubby grab for cash.

Some geographers, of course, have been sensitive to this issue of engagement and relevance. There is an alternative history of human geography to be written in which the concern of such historical figures as Karl Wittfogel, Jean Jacques Reclus, and Peter Kropotkin merge into the writings of such contemporary figures as Bill Bunge, Peter Gould, David Harvey, David Smith, and Ron Johnston. In this alternative tradition, one of social concern and social criticism, a consistent theme has been the need for a people's geography, for an intellectual exercise sensitive to social injustice, political realities, and economic power, yet powered by a belief in the possibility of emancipatory theory and liberating practice. This emancipatory impulse appears again and again in geography, partly in response to wider social changes, partly as a reaction against the incorporation of the discipline into the agenda of the establishment, and partly as the result of an individual's need to say something about pressing questions of social importance and political consequence. The issues echo down the years. In 1885 Peter Kropotkin was writing about the need for a geographical education to combat nationalism and racism; one hundred years later, political geographers continue to make the same plea. This chapter is an attempt to celebrate, consolidate, and codify this alternative impulse. In it I want to raise the fundamental question, geography for whom? and to provide a "charter" for a progressive human geography.

A Question of Purpose

To create a progressive human geography is to beg the question, what is a progressive human geography? Human geography is progressive, I feel, when it is an emancipatory activity. What do I mean by emancipatory? The word, first of all, suggests a number of things we should be doing—combating war, helping in the fight against repressive regimes, resisting oppressive practices that destroy the biosphere or that discriminate against people on the grounds of race, gender, class, and age. We can agree on this. The difficulties arise in the detailed agenda we adopt for our "progressive human geography." I do not wish to set down a list of dos and don'ts. I do, however, want to raise the issue for debate. In terms of broad areas of research, let me mention the following.

The Appearance of People

In 1970 the geographer Torsten Hägerstrand asked the question, "what about people in regional science?". The issue keeps reappearing. In 1977 David Smith called for

> a new paradigm for geography. Its essential nature humanistic
> . . . a people geography about real people, and *for* the people in
> the sense of contributing to the enlargement of human being for
> all . . . devoted to human freedom (Smith 1977, 370).

In his 1984 address to the Institute of British Geographers, David Harvey echoed this theme in his call for

> a peoples' geography, not based on pious universalism, ideals
> and good intents, but on a more mundane enterprise that re-
> flects earthly interests and claims, that confronts ideologies and
> prejudice (Harvey 1984, 7).

The reiteration of this demand has been a product of the dehumanizing of human geography—people have either been ignored in structural overdetermination or lost in statistical abstractions. As a corrective the humanists and phenomenologists have stressed the importance of human agency. But we also need to ask *which* people for *whose* geography? There is a need for an analysis of those people marginalized by and in society. More marginalized groups include women, racialized minorities, the young, the elderly, and physically and mentally challenged groups. Although race and racism have gained sympathetic coverage, there is still only scant attention paid to the young, the elderly, and people with disabilities or mental illness. The inclusion of such groups into our studies can prompt new questions and methods of study (as has been the case in feminist geography) as well as illuminate vital dimensions of the experience of economic, social, and political change. Marginalized groups present not only a subject of study; but to understand the how, where, when, and why of the very process of marginalization is vital to a progressive human geography. We need to examine in more detail how the needs of certain groups are prioritized while others are ignored in the conscious and unconscious making and remaking of our human geographies.

Politics

A more explicit recognition of the role of politics in structuring the subject matter of our discipline and of the part that geography can play in wider political practice is long overdue. Research has, for too long and sometimes unwittingly, been related to the needs of government; and research areas are often dictated by current political fads and fashions.

The importance of the different forces shaping our discipline is well illustrated with reference to political geography and in particular the life and writings of Mackinder and Kropotkin. Sir Halford John Mackinder was a leading figure in the development of geography in the United Kingdom. In his writings and public duties, he gave intellectual substance to English patriotism and

British imperialism. Born into the middle class, he became a member of the establishment committed to the existing order and the British state. Peter Kropotkin (1842–1921), in contrast, was born into the aristocracy of czarist Russia but became an anarchist and social critic of the existing order. While he was secretary of the Imperial Russian Geographical Society in 1874, he was arrested but escaped to England in 1876. He developed theories of mutual cooperation. These two men stand at the opposite ends of an engaged human geography. One, a servant of the ruling class, saw his geographical writings as "an aid to statecraft" and in particular the needs of an imperial Britain. The other spread the ideas of "No-Government, of the rights of the individual, of local action, and free agreement—as against those of State almightiness, centralization, and discipline" (Kropotkin 1978, 337). Mackinder developed his ideas as an intellectual tool for the British state, whereas Kropotkin proclaimed his principles of mutual cooperation and decentralization as aids to human emancipation. While Mackinder saw a geographic education as essential if the "educated classes" were not "to lose their grip and their influence over the half-educated proletariat" (Mackinder 1921, 383), Kropotkin had a very different view:

> The task of geography in early childhood [is] to interest the child in the great phenomena of nature, to awaken the desire of knowing and explaining them. Geography must render, moreover, another far more important service, it must teach us . . . that we are all brethren, whatever our nationality . . . geography must . . . counterbalance hostile influences—a means of dissipating . . . prejudice and of creating other feelings more worthy of humanity. It must show that each nationality brings its own precious building stone for the general development of the commonwealth, and that only small parts of each nation are in-

terested in maintaining national hatreds and jealousies (Kropotkin 1885, 942).

Geography lost its way when it followed Mackinder rather than Kropotkin. In the early history of political geography, it was the tradition of Mackinder that dominated the scene. Political geography became an aid to statecraft bound up with the demands of state governments. Today if we are to serve an international community in the pursuit of a global order of peace and to convert a discipline of war into a project for peace, then it is to Kropotkin we should turn for intellectual succor and historical precedence rather than to Mackinder and the legacy of geopolitics.

An Ecological Awareness

Recent years have witnessed a revival of earlier concerns with environmentalism and ecology. In the late 1960s and 1970s such concerns found their place in a search for relevance within the geographical discipline, but in subsequent years the concepts of environmentalism and ecology have been relegated to the subdiscipline of physical geography or to the back benches of environmental "interface" courses pursued by undergraduate students. This separation of human geography from explicit ecological concern, naïve in the past, has become ludicrous and dooms us to further marginalization. Despite current skepticism that some "green" issues may have negative as well as positive features, the time is right for bringing issues of society and environment together in a "green human geography" that considers global concerns and national issues as well as more parochial conflicts.

It is a sad paradox that human geography has lost its environmental sensitivity just as environmental concerns are reemerging as issues of major significance. An awareness of environmental spaces and ecological places need to be rewoven into the fabric of our subject, and attention to such themes could provide the basis for a stronger and more coherent discipline as well as encourage deeper and more qualitative examinations of what is progress.

The Geography of Progressive Activities

Many embryonic local "bases of resistance" have developed against the restructuring policies being pushed through by central governments and multinational corporations. Some are directed primarily at making demands of the local or national state and are broadly consumption-oriented; others are centered on the creation of local-level alternatives, especially in the production sphere. From workers' cooperatives to self-build groups to resident action groups there is a variety of acts of resistance and sites of struggle. A human geography of such progressive activities would provide a valuable stimulation to a progressive human geography.

A Matter of Method

A truly human geography also requires the utilization of a progressive methodology. This involves the use of a rich variety of methods, including much more qualitative, interpretive, ethnographic methods to portray the personal circumstances and inner life of different societies and people. Not only is the use of such methods arguably more sympathetic to the human beings involved in our study but also methods of an ethnographic nature allow us to experiment with new and different ways of presenting our work. We are currently restricted by the historical legacy of the quantitative revolution, which demands that each and every apprentice geographer be put through an assault course in "rigor" and an introduction to statistical method. Such lessons are of course valid, but their emphasis at the expense of so-called softer options means that the progress of geography is restricted.

A word of warning. There has been a revival of ethnographic research methods in human geography in recent years. Too much of it, to my mind, ignores the structural context of people's lives and concentrates overmuch on the poor. There is much less work on the rich and powerful. This bias reflects power. Academics have easier access to the poor than to the rich. They gain deference from one and and tend to be ignored by the other. To use only ethnograhic methodologies on the poor is a form of exploitation made all the more hypocritical by the sanctimonious nature of academic posturing. Qualitative research is too important to be left to academics reinforcing their position by interviewing only those poorer and less powerful than themselves.

Many observers have identified a gap that has consistently occurred, in geography specifically and in social science more generally, between people's lives and academic theories.

> Much of what passes for theory fails to connect with the lives that people lead, whereas most descriptive social surveys too often fail to grasp the structure of social relations and the sense which people make of them. It is almost as if another way of writing has to be developed: something which "tells it like it is . . . ," which destroys the gap between the abstract (Nichols and Benyon 1977, 7).

We need another way of looking, another way of writing.

How do we go about doing a progressive human geography? Let me make a number of suggestions.

If we use a plurality of methods, we are more likely to be sensitive to different individual and group perceptions, resources, and abilities. A progressive human geography, then, neither dismisses nor denies structural factors but allows a range of voices to speak. There is a need for polyvocal and polylocal strategies that consider different voices in different places.

Ultimately, we need to consider the production of our work and its reproduction and dissemination. Our discourse has to be widened. There is a long tradition of popular and populist writing in human geography, still evident in such publications as *National Geographic* and *The Geographical Magazine*. But elsewhere (and particularly in reviews) the description "journalistic" appears as a (thinly) veiled criticism. The institutionalization of our discipline has brought a level of professionalism but too often at the cost of a closed discourse. Geographers need to open out to and influence a popular audience. We need to write well. In this regard perhaps we could follow the example of the better journalists who write in an accessible style. We need to develop the concept of *reportage*—a form of committed writing—to collapse the division between observer and observed. The "analytical other" as a disciplinary role model sometimes needs to be replaced by the "committed other."

But before we open up the discussion, we have to be sure that we have something relevant and important to say. To do this we need to overcome the discouragement of personal experience relevant in academic writing; adopt alternative textual strategies, such as direct use of interview material, audio, and visual tapes; and generate our own theories rather than rely on the reified theoretical other.

We live in interesting times. The world order is changing. The old bipolar structure of competing superpowers has collapsed. Fundamental questions about the role and shape of the state are being raised. Environmental issues are back on the political agenda. Our individual lives are subject to constant and accelerating change. As academics we have a duty and a responsibility to make a contribution to this shifting terrain of argument and debate. As social scientists we have to make some kind of order from the chaos. As geographers we have a special responsibility to make sense of the ambiguities and polarities involved in the relationship between people and environment, space and place, the social and the spatial, the structural and the personal. If we are to fulfill this role, the notion of progress *for* human geographers needs to be replaced by a conception of progress *by* human geographers and *in* human geography. The task is immense, and the problems are many; but I can think of no more exciting intellectual project than the construction of a progressive human geography.

6

Mythos, Logos, and Community

In 1671 the English physician, mathematician, and inventor Robert Hooke (1635–1703), considered by many the greatest mechanic of his age, started a diary. He called it *Memoranda*. The pages of the first nine months are divided into two parts: on the left-hand side, he kept a record of weather conditions; on the right he made a more personal commentary of the day's events, his feelings, and all those private things that we associate with the term *diary*.

Hooke was writing at an important time. In 1660 the Royal Society was founded. Its full title was the Royal Society of London for Improving Natural Knowledge. It was granted a royal charter and thus formal recognition in 1662. Hooke, an early secretary of the Royal Society, played a pivotal role during a crucial period when science was being defined as a separate discourse.

Hooke is best known to us today for his scientific endeavors, which are considerable. He devised a telegraph system, invented the screw-divided quadrant and the spiral spring that powers watches, constructed telescopes and arithmetic machines, formulated the law of elasticity, which is given his name, and anticipated the law of gravitation.

What is of interest to me is how one side of Hooke's *Memoranda* has come to dominate our stories. We tell stories to each other. Children are told stories by their parents. Parents tell stories to each other. Governments tell stories to their citizens and to other governments.

Communities can be distinguished by the type of stories they tell to each other. The most marginalized groups and individuals are those with no voice; they have no stories to tell or audiences to listen. To tell your story is to give meaning to your life. To lose your voice, to have no story, is to lose meaning, significance. Importance is given to those with the most powerful stories. Power is a struggle for whose stories dominate, which stories are told, and what stories are "true."

The word *story* has a fairy-tale feel to it. A fiction, a child's thing, a product of imagination, something from Hollywood. Something not quite real. That's why I want to use it. And to extend it.

Science used to be seen, and is still seen by many, as an enterprise driven by rational considerations. We are now much more aware of the sociology of the production of knowledge and its link with the powerful groups that set the agenda for scientific endeavors. Much has been written about the scientific method. Its development and refinement are seen as the basis for scientific achievement. It has led to increased knowledge of the world. More recent criticisms focus on the dangers of a method abstracted from moral concerns or devoid of social considerations. The scientific method gave us penicillin. It also gave us nuclear weapons.

Science is storytelling. The scientific method is just one way of telling a story. There are others: fairy tales, novels, films, and all those things associated with the term *text*. To use the term *text* is to activate a whole battery of themes from death of the author to deconstructionism via postmodernism and political correctness. Let me continue to keep it simple by referring to these as stories.

Stories are made up of words. In Greek there are two meanings of *word*: mythos and logos.

Mythos is a story both individual and general. It seeks to make sense of what is unknown or unknowable; it is narrative in structure, full of moral resonance. *Logos* is concerned with words whose validity can be argued or proven. It is the embodiment of reason and rationality.

Mythos is concerned with eternal truths, logos with the measurement of change. Logos persuades the mind, mythos appeals to the heart. One refers to the left-hand side of Hooke's *Memoranda*, the other echoes the right-hand side.

There are other resonances that circulate around this dichotomy. Table 6.1 indicates the main points. The table has a graphic rhetoric. The two columns can be seen as twin pillars of the house of communication. Under the general term *mythos* can be found emotion, commitment, wisdom, and the sense of recurring cycles and eternal mysteries. Under *logos* can be found objectivity, intellect, the emphasis on change, and the concern with problem solving.

The distinction is a rhetorical device. The dichotomies are rarely so stark and divisive. Even the most abstract intellectual discourses can be suffused with a passion, a wisdom, and a concern with truth and engagement. And even the most artistic concerns can be mechanical, unfeeling, dispassionate, and disengaged. Much of modern art, for example, lost its passion and merely gained technique.

Table 6.1

Mythos and Logos

Mythos	Logos
particular-universal	general-specific
place	space
experienced	transmitted
wisdom	knowledge
truth	information
emotion	intellect
cycle	changes
engagement	objective
mystery	problem

Rebecca's Story

Rather than see mythos and logos as competing paradigms, we should, I believe, see them as alternative and complementary ways of telling stories. Some people are more comfortable with telling only a certain kind of story. They should refrain, however, from seeing their storytelling as the only storytelling or as the only legitimate form of storytelling. They are both part of the same broad attempt to make sense of our world, to give shape and meaning to our experience. They are connected, intimately related, balanced to form a complete whole, like the brain with its right and left sides each doing different things but both spheres combining to form an integral unit. The brain metaphor is reflected and mapped onto Hooke's spatial division of his *Memoranda*. A single page divided into two halves, one observational, one more reflective, both a product of the same mind.

A broad division can be made in how we interact with the world. Some have a need to empathize, whereas others have a tendency to abstract. Anthony Storr (1988, 89–91) summarizes a large body of psychological literature concerned with this distinction. He quotes the study of schoolboys by Liam Hudson, which identified *divergers* and *convergers*. Divergers were attracted to the softer sciences and did less well in conventional intelligence tests. The convergers were attracted to the hard sciences and did very well in intelligence tests where there was one undisputed answer. In his work on children, Howard Gardner (1980, 47) identified *dramatists* and *patterners*. Dramatists engaged more in storytelling, conversation, and pretend play. The patterners were drawn to drawing, modeling, and the arrangement of numerical arrays. This dichotomy is extended by Jerome Bruner (1986, 36–39) into two modes of thought: the narrative and the paradigmatic. Again and again we see this basic distinction.

In an interesting study, Oliver Sacks (1987) tells the story of Rebecca. She was just nineteen when she was referred to his clinic. She had a cleft palate and little sight and was painfully shy and so lacking in coordination that one doctor described her as a "motor moron." She could not open a door with a key and sometimes spent as much as hour trying to fit a hand or foot into the wrong glove or shoe. As a paradigmatic being, she was by common consensus a misfit, a failure, a figure of ridicule, an object of pity. Rebecca was sent to a number of standard development classes. These were a failure. They only showed her how little she knew. They reinforced the limits of her self.

She had a love of the theater and eventually joined a theater workshop. She was transformed. She loved the drama, the stories; she could perform in the narrative mode with ease and sophistication. The "motor moron" became a gifted actress with a skill and poise in speech and body movements that belied her former self. The paradigmatic failure was a narrative success. The unsuccessful patterner was a successful dramatist. In the world of logos she was a misfit, but in the world of mythos she could move with grace and beauty. Just as people with no sight develop acute hearing, so a damaged logos may create fertile conditions for an exceptional mythos.

Community

Stories imply listeners as well as speakers, an audience as well as performers. Let me repeat an earlier sentence. *What is of interest to me is how one side of Hooke's* Memoranda *has come to dominate our stories.* Who is the *our?* Who tells the story, and who listens?

Here I will look at only one of many. Let us consider the academic community. Academics have both an advantage and a disadvantage. The advantage is that academics can tell stories for a living. They give lectures and write articles and books. They have access to the cultural means of reproduction. The disadvantage is that they have the freedom to write without being read. Academic articles and books are more often cited than read. Literacy and intelligibility are declining virtues as the conventions of our genres make us more and more unintelligible to the nonspecialist. Perhaps we gain focus, but at the cost of connection. Our audience becomes more sophisticated as it shrinks in size. We need to ask the question, who is our audience? What is the community of tellers and listeners?

Different types of stories are told to different types of audience. Academic stories have just as many conventions as the fairy story. For "once upon a time" we can insert "recent studies suggest" and for "they all lived happily ever after" we can put "further research is necessary."

As academics we have to ask the question, to whom should we be telling our stories? Who is our community of listeners? If it is just to each other, then we run the risk of social and political irrelevancy. If we tell the stories only to the rich and powerful, then we fail in our moral obligations. But even if we can engage a wider, broader audience, we have to then ask the question: What kind of stories should we be telling?

The New Geography of the 1960s was an attempt to introduce logos into our stories. Geography borrowed from economics and physics, the natural sciences, and the hard social sciences. From the 1980s onward, there was the postmodern backlash. Geography imported from the humanities and especially literary theory. Metanarrative was out, deconstructing the text was in. At best an attempt to reintroduce mythos, at worst just one career advancement bandwagon. The debate became polarized, the two camps on either side of the page. Mythos and logos became separated. In one sense the shifts, for all their mean-spirited acrimony, were shifts of correction. The dominance of logos generated the resurgence of mythos. Geography seems to straddle the middle ground between these two sets of stories. This is not to claim imperial preeminence for one academic discipline. It is to suggest that on the boundary between the sciences and the humanities, geography is particularly sensitive to such corrective shifts. To argue which one is superior is to miss the point entirely. It is to replace a debate with a schism, an arena of permanent and incessant interaction with a court of law searching for the guilty.

We need both mythos and logos. Individual scholars, being individuals, will favor one over the other. Their background, training, and personal predilection will lead them to rely on one more than the other. What I want to stress, the moral of this story so to speak, is that there is more than one way to tell a story.

7

Postmodernity, Space, and Place

The "Myth" of Postmodernity

There is a new myth. It goes something like this:

Once upon a time there was something called modernism. This was the thing that came before postmodernism. It consisted of a belief in rationality and progress. It had a concern with uncovering universal truths and transcendent values. Its two dominant religions were Science and Marxism. Postmodernism, the thing that came after modernism, is a concern with uniqueness, a distrust of metanarratives.

I call this a myth rather than a hypothesis or argument because it is not so much an examination of the history of social thought as a morality tale; and like all good morality tales, it has right and wrong, good and bad. Postmodern epistemology, so it is argued, has greater sensitivity to the local, the unique, the ephemeral. Postmodernism, although there are some qualifiers to be made, is a "Good Thing."

The myth has the enormous advantage of being simple, clear,

110

and easily understandable. Like all myths it is not so much wrong as partial and selective. Let me mention just two of the "silences." The first is the obvious need to tell a selective story. Thus discussions of Marxism fail to mention the cultural materialism of Raymond Williams or the political sophistication of Antonio Gramsci. Both authors refuse the categorization of economic determinists or structural Marxists and thus fail to register in the myth. Similarly, science is associated with positivism, an easy target, which allows a simple dismissal of science. No mention here of Heisenberg's principle of uncertainty, the relativism of the Einsteinian view of the world, or the connections drawn between science and religion by such physicists as Paul Davies. The second silence concerns the shift from modernism to postmodernism. Why the shift? When? Where? If the eager postmodernists are so keen on contingencies, specificities, and locale, the shift is rarely given a reason, a time, a place, or a broader social significance. The myth hardens a historically and place-specific process into a placeless, timeless before and after. On closer examination modernism and postmodernism may just be academic terms for then and now, past and present, yesterday and today.

Despite its silences, and all discourses have silences, the postmodern debate cannot be easily dismissed. The postmodern critique raises important issues of representation. One of the questions for geographers in the New Geography of the 1960s was, is it possible to represent people and things from small samples? The question in the 1990s is, can anything be represented? The answer is yes, but at a price. Representation is never complete and it is never innocent. We tell stories to each other, but the language we use in our stories, and the way we tell our stories all play a part in the production and consumption of knowledge. Making sure our stories are multilocal and polyvocal does help, not so much to eliminate the bias but to highlight the bias in representation that affects us all. We can neither hide from this bias (a solution of some modernists) nor assume we can eradicate it (the goal of some postmodernists).

There is a condition of change in the world, a fundamental restructuring. At all levels. The new world order. The new capitalism. Post-Marxism. Postfeminism. New Man. The recent terms with their emphasis on post- and new all give a clue that the world is changing. We know what we are leaving behind, but we are not so sure of where we are going. Postmodernism is as good a descriptive term as any to indicate the uncertainty.

Two major schools of thought can be identified. There are those who argue that nothing much has changed or that, if it has, the old ways can still be used. These are the *reluctant modernists*. Then there are the *enthusiastic postmodernists*; those who say that was then, this is now, a whole new way of looking at the world is required. I would put myself in the agnostic middle as someone who feels the winds of change but worries about the silences of the myth. To ignore the work of a Raymond Williams or an Antonio Gramsci or to equate science with positivism offends me. Similarly, I feel that a defense of the old modernism is difficult if not impossible. I not so much embrace postmodernism as I don't have any alternative at the moment. So my view is a provisional, pragmatic decision, not the religious conversion that seems all the rage. If a tag is required, then reluctant postmodernist would be as good as any.

In this new debate, human geography has an important role to play. All locations are both spaces and places. They are connected to national and global circuits of power, money, and influence. They are also locales where people live, get by, make connections and, reproduce their social lives. Places are full of cultural meaning and significance. The old regional geography was concerned with identifying the uniqueness of place. The New Geography of the 1960s was concerned with the spatial organization of society and concentrated on the space element of locations. Much of the Marxist-inspired work examined how places were subject to the same economic influences, how the world was a giant chessboard with capital and labor making move and countermove. The reaction to this concern with space has been to concentrate on the place element, the local, the unique, and the vernacular. Witness the renewed interest in cultural geography. This is an important and necessary countertrend that I welcome. We need to balance space with place, however. Barney Warf (1993), an enthusiastic postmodernist, writes, "a theory of poverty in New York is *fundamentally* different from a theory of poverty in London" (italics mine). This may be a rhetorical flourish. Something I am not immune from. But if he actually believes this and if this represents a more general trend, then I am worried. I can accept that poverty is different in different countries and different cities, because the experience varies by time and place and person. Discussions of poverty need to reflect such differences. But if we are going to try to generate fundamentally different theories about poverty in two capitalist cities, then perhaps we need to redefine the word *theory*. If we refuse to speculate on the connection between poverty in the two cities, then we restrict ourselves; we limit our capacity to generate interesting ideas and influence important debates. The real challenge is to combine both place and space, the general and the particular, the vernacular and the universal. Global trends of commodification, market penetration, and standardization of forms of cultural consumption are both adopted and resisted around the world. There is a mosaic of acceptance and rejection that both binds and separates people and locations. It is the intersection between the global and the local, the universal and the vernacular, place and space that contains the ambiguity and paradoxes of the contemporary world. If we look only at space, we ignore the local; and if we look only at place, we fail to make the connections. The postmodern debate should generate strategies and methods for handling this complexity. If it merely polarizes into before and after the Fall, good guys and bad guys, the modernists in black hats and postmodernists in white hats, then we will have missed a marvelous opportunity.

To look only at the universals of space was the blindness of modernism. To consider only the places of the local is the silence of postmodernism.

Researching Space and Place

Space and place are well-known names that refer to ideas of immense importance; let me use some examples. The "inner city" is a space, Brixton a place; the "Third World" is a space, Dacca a place. Space is abstracted, place is particular, one is a mental construct, the other a social construct, both an environmental context that reflects, influences, and records social life.

It is the point of contact between space and place that is providing the most fruitful scope for the geographical enterprise and for wider significance. The division of place and space condenses the dichotomies of subject and object, theory and fact, structure and process. We need a dialectical sensitivity to handle these ambiguities. If our studies are too specific, more concerned with place than space, then they are too parochial to see the wider social relations. If they become too abstracted, more related to a general space than to particular places, they become free-floating comments lacking points of contact with the world around us. To see the spatial implications of place and to be aware of the platial consequence of space are difficult tasks. I want to flag three particular problems.

Discouragement of Personal Experience

Academics are like members of a contemporary priesthood who have to perform rites of passage (the Ph.D.) to gain entry and repeat ritual acts to maintain their status (e.g., publishing articles). In both cases the rituals have become dominated by a particular form of writing. In contemporary literary theory, the death of the author with the discovery of the creative reader caused and continues to cause quite a stir. I don't know why because in academic writing the author seems to have been dead for years. Not only is the *I* studiously avoided by most academics, but the writer is not supposed to make any important statement without the ritual accompaniment of references. The conspiracy is maintained by the referees of academic journals who regularly tell the editors and the authors that this or that paper has not cited all the appropriate sources. There is a real need for refereeing, and proper criticism is a valuable device to prevent our currency of ideas from being debased or counterfeited; but it has now reached the level of ancestor-worship, where anything significant in the text needs the authority of others. The system downgrades the authenticity of our own experience.

Too often in the pursuit of the goal of objective observer, academic writing becomes dry, boring, lifeless, and dull. It lacks the lifeblood of personal experience and the presence of a committed "I." There is a lack of moral purpose in too much of our writing. This lack of sympathy is reflected in our treatment of people and places. By denying the legitimacy of our experiences, we lack the ability to comprehend fully the experiential nature of places. This is not a plea for more behavioral- or phenomenological-type studies because many of these have the same exploitative relationship with people and places as more positivist research. To say something about the peopling of places, we need to allow room for our experience of particular places.

The Tyranny of the Text

Combining space and place is a difficult task made more difficult by the nature of the linear text that most of us use. The written word is a marvelous form of communication, but it often lacks the creative linking of diverse threads available in the montage and collage of the moving image or the spoken word. The written text has a tendency to impose a linear narrative, which makes it difficult to combine theory and observations, general and particular, space and place. To counter this difficulty, we need to consider alternative textual strategies and find new ways of "writing." Geographers have always been familiar with maps. As a form of communication, the map seems to be going out of fashion. We need to encourage its use along with the use of tapes and videos. Maps are a graphic script that allows another dimension to the linear flow of written text. Developing another form of writing involves cultivating old tools and new technologies. You can imagine how enlightening a study of finance capital on urban structure would be if it included taped interviews with a small investor, a pension-fund manager, a dweller of a house threatened with demolition, and a building worker. Careful editing would be able to present the kaleidoscope of cross-currents, implications, and processes just as successfully if not more so than a paper of closely written text. Some of the best work in social science is being done by radio and television journalists. They think, unlike most academics, that important issues can be presented in an attractive and accessible fashion. I look forward to the days when a Ph.D. can be submitted in the form of a tape or a video as well as a text. A variety of textual strategies will enable us to link spaces with places.

Fear of Theory

The segmentation of most academic papers with the theory bit at the beginning followed by empirical observations is not just because of the linearity of written texts. There is both a worship and a fear of Theory in Britain and North America. In the last twenty-five years Theory has become sexy and successful, and social theorists and their translators have gained wider credibility and academic success. Grand theories have been imported. And like good wine, it has snob value if it is foreign and labeled with a difficult name. A cynic might suggest that favored theorists are those with foreign names that are difficult to say, for example, Foucault and Althusser because their "proper" pronunciation allows aficionados to recognize each other. This is not to denigrate theory or European theorists. It is simply to note that they are too often used to impress more than enlighten. Theory with a capital *T* has become something difficult, accessible only to the skilled reader, only to those clever enough to master the cunning cleverness of Marx, unravel the ambiguities of Foucault, or unpack the full implications of Habermas. In much of human geography, as in other disciplines Theory has become someone else's work, something related to space that you take with you into places in a top-down, ready-made way. Fear is maintained by treating theory as difficult and seeing theorizing as an activity best left to the great name. There has been a growing division of labor with status implications between the theorists and the empirical researchers. Places are not allowed to generate theories; they have become the testing ground for theories with the result that the full connections between space and place are never fully recovered. To begin recovering these connections, we should begin to demystify Theory and theorizing by teaching our students and ourselves that we all have the capacity for theorizing. We are all social theorists.

We should not need to rely always on the "theoretical other" to make meaningful statements about place and space.

Some "Modest Proposals"

Academic writers have the greatest freedom—to write without being read. It is a sobering thought that most of our written work is never read. It is even more disheartening to discover that most of it was never meant to be read. It has become an enforced ritual, vital for promotion prospects, necessary to maintain status. Most academic papers are counters to be collected then cashed in for tenure, promotion, a professorship: they are unconnected to a readership. Lacking a critical, interactive readership, too much of our writing has become ossified into a sterile rut of brief theoretical review, empirical bit, then conclusion all wrapped up with an impressive list of mostly unread references. I don't have any immediate solution to the publish-or-perish syndrome; but if we have to write, we can at least try to make the publications more interesting, more vital, and, just maybe, more influential in public debates. Here are just three proposals:

- Making public our private obsessions with our work and allowing personal experience to be presented rather than negated.
- Devising alternative textual strategies to the written text, involving the greater use of maps, recordings, and videos.
- Generating theories as much on the basis of our own experiences with people and places as with the writings of others.

We are involved in a collective endeavor. Scholarship is a group activity, albeit pursued by individuals. We need the work and ideas of others. But the habit of ignoring the "I," downgrading our own voice, our own experiences, and our own thoughts has become a fetish. Referencing and citation have become a system of oppression, not an enhancement of creativity.

The ideas of others should liberate our own thoughts, not replace them.

8

Geographers as Resident Aliens

Tom Weller is a neighbor of mine who lives in Upstate New York. When he first heard me speak with my Scottish vowels, he said, "You are not from these parts." He was right.

I arrived to live in New York State from Reading, Britain, in December 1990. When the plane landed, I thought there must have been a pilot error. Surely we had landed in Alaska or Iceland. Two feet of snow and subzero temperatures. No mistake . . . it was Syracuse, New York.

After I recovered from the shock of driving on the wrong side of roads covered over with snow and ice in a car without four-wheel drive—the experience is scarred in my memory as well as my car—I wanted to go to work. I wanted to study Syracuse. This has been a habit of mine. Part of my work has always consisted of studying the place I am in. At graduate school in Bristol, my Ph.D. thesis was an analysis of the local housing market. When I moved to Reading, I looked at the process of capital investment and community struggle over the local built environment. And when I was in Australia, I looked at aboriginal painting as well as office development in Sydney.

To study Syracuse was part of a recurring theme of my work. But more than just my work. It was an important part of my life. We are driven in our lives as in our work by obsessions. One of mine has been the need to understand where I am. I have been obsessed for over twenty years with the need to make sense of the world around me and to impose some kind of order, fleeting though it may be, on the constant flux of life around me. As geographers we have the opportunity to study places; as academics we have the legitimation to work through our obsessions; as scholars we have a duty to communicate to others; as human beings we have the need to discover our world and ourselves.

To study a new place is to be in the position of outsider. As an outsider I have advantages: I have limited knowledge, I do not take things for granted, I have not yet internalized the taken-for-granted world of the locals; I come from somewhere else. This means I have a different yardstick to evaluate new places.

We do not stay outsiders for long. In Syracuse I learned to say gas and hood rather than petrol and bonnet and also discovered that a slam dunk is not a move in judo.

But we should resist total incorporation. We need to tread a finely drawn, precarious line between being what I will refer to as, on the one hand, *permanent outsiders* and, on the other, as *incorporated locals*. As permanent outsiders we run the risk of superficiality, a lack of connection, a distancing from the everyday concerns of the community. As incorporated locals we can easily lose the sense of wonder at what is around us, take for granted the importance of the local place, and lose sight of the mystery and the magic of where we are.

It is a difficult line to draw because it embodies, condenses, and encapsulates other polarities:

- Distance and engagement.
- Compassion and analysis.
- Objectivity and commitment.
- Them and us.
- You and me.

When Tom Weller said I was not from these parts, there was an implied question. Where are you from? The answer is . . . it depends. I have found my status change over time and through space. Who we are is a function of where we are.

I did not realize I was Scots until I went to graduate school in England. When I went there, people said I had an "accent." It was my first experience of being Otherized. There have been others:

In Australia I was a "bloody pommy."

In other places I have been described as a white male.

When I was playing soccer in England during one particularly vicious game, I could see the opposition coach point to me and hear him shout, *"Someone get the little Irish bastard!"* The *little* was not so bad, nor the *bastard*, but I really objected to the *Irish*.

Geography is not only the study of places. Like all disciplines it can reveal much about ourselves. My experience of different places has been part of an academic enterprise but also something more.

The study of places has also been an unconscious act of self-revelation and a vital part in the forging of my identity.

In late August 1992, I had a change of status. The US Immigration Service granted me a "green card," which allows me to stay and work in the United States. Like most things it is not what it says. It is not green and its not much of a card. It is a very small red piece of plastic. Across the top of the card above the picture of me that makes me look like a convicted drug dealer in bold blue ink are the words, RESIDENT ALIEN.

I like the ambiguity. I am resident here but an alien. An insider but an outsider. Engaged yet distanced, connected yet separate. The term has a significance beyond its narrow legal definition. Perhaps we should all become, figuratively at least, resident aliens. Not incorporated locals or permanent outsiders but resident aliens.

Perhaps the best human geography is done by resident aliens, those able to connect and reconnect, involve and engage, commit to the local yet see the global. Human geographers as resident aliens have the ability to connect the global with the local, the present with the past, them with us, you with me.

Part Three

Postmodernity

9

Setting the Scene

There are some words and ideas that sort of sneak up on you. I cannot remember the first time I heard the word *postmodern*. But before I knew it, the word was everywhere. It was a noun, an adjective, the subject of academic conferences and infighting, reported in glossy magazines, emanating from the mouths of Hollywood actors as well as law professors, quoted by advertising executives, designers, architects, and writers. Lots of people. It had become one of those ideas whose time had come.

The word and the idea behind it reflect a sense that the world is changing. The term implies a change from modern to postmodern with its implicit notation that we know what we are leaving, but we are unsure where we are going. Some see the trend everywhere, others see it nowhere but in the minds of cultural commentators building their reputations in assigning deep theories to shallow events. The word *postmodern* mirrors our uncertainty, gives label to our worry (hope) that something is happening to our world and our understanding of it, our representation of it. Our vision of society, history, and knowledge is being undermined, transformed, deeply disturbed.

I knew the word *postmodern* was important and long lasting when many began to say it was a shallow and ephemeral trend.

I also knew it was not going to last forever when others described it as the next major epoch of civilization.

A closer look revealed that there were as many definitions as people using the word. This part of the book is my attempt to make some kind of sense of the idea; it is a guide for the curious written by the perplexed.

This section uses an old device, an A to Z. If postmodernism is about the decline of the big story, the death of the metanarrative, then it didn't seem right to write a book with a standard narrative structure. Hence, this format that has the advantage of allowing a multiplicity of readings. A postmodern book about postmodernity. Individual readers are much freer to make their own narrative by the way and order in which they read the entries. There are as many narratives as readers. There is no beginning, big middle, and flourishing climax. It is a mosaic, to be read in any order. It is your order.

10

An A to Z of Postmodernity

Entries

A   AIDS   Anxiety   Architecture   Authenticity   Author

B   Baldness   Beach   Biodegradable   Body

C   Capitalism   Cohort   Cold War   Commodification

D   Decolonization   Deconstructionism   Discourse
Disneyland

E   Enlightenment   Environment

F   Family   Feminism   Film

G   Gender   Glasgow   Global Village   God

H   Holocaust

I   Image   Industrial   Intellectual

J   Japan   Jeans

K   Kurds

L   Lifestyle

M   Marxism   Modernism   Modernity   Multiculturalism
Museums

129

N   Nationalism   New Age   New Man   Nouvelle Cuisine

O   Office   Ozone

P   Patriarchy   Political Correctness   Postmodern
     Postmodernity

Q   Quilt

R   Race   Religion

S   Science   Self   Semiotics   Sexuality   Superficial

T   Text   Television   Third World   Truth

U   United States

V   Vernacular

W   Wall Street   Westerns

Y   Yuppies

Z   Zapper

AIDS

AIDS is short for acquired immune deficiency syndrome. It shares the characteristic of many new things first given a name by scientists, like refrigerator or television. Once these things are used by ordinary people, the name becomes shortened to something more usable, like fridge or TV. The long name for the disease was soon shortened to its acronym.

Some hellfire moralists may see it as a scourge for permissiveness or as a punishment against homosexuals; but for most of us, AIDS is a threat, a fear, a shadow whose power is exaggerated by its connection with the body, sexuality, and desire. AIDS has changed the whole nature of sexual relations.

AIDS is a product of the 1980s. It was probably around for a much longer time but was first identified in 1981. We now know that AIDS is caused by the human immunodeficiency virus (HIV). You can get this through sexual intercourse, by injection, and by transfusion of blood. We don't know how or where it started; we don't, as yet, have a cure. The search for the cure is the sort of adventure that allows science and scientists to wield some authority and power at a time when science is getting a bad press.

AIDS quickly spread. It is now of epidemic proportions. A few thousand cases in the early 1980s; estimates suggest numbers of between 35 million and 100 million by the year 2000. If the upper estimates are correct, by the end of the century AIDS will be the single biggest cause of death in the world. The late modern age had the threat of nuclear destruction as its Armageddon. The postmodern world has AIDS as one of its collective fears.

Anxiety

You can tell an age as much by its silences as its utterances.

The modern age was a difficult time for the intelligentsia. The Lonely Crowd, The Age of Anxiety, The Homeless Mind. These were epithets for the modern era. Anxiety was the modern condition. The decline of religion and the loss of tradition severed people from the warm comfort and solid foundations of traditional belief. Life for the sensitive was like living in a Beckett play, a hopeless search for meaning in a meaningless universe.

If Samuel Beckett is an example of a modern intellectual, then the postmodern equivalent is Walt Disney. Who cares about meaning as long as you are having a good time? No longer the incessant search for authenticity in life or in art, make your own fun rides, construct your own Main Street.

Anxiety, as a much-debated social condition rather than a personal experience, is now a thing of the past. There are still anxious people. Angst has not disappeared. But it is no longer such a defining condition of the age.

Choice caused anxiety. To have the opportunity to choose meant the opportunity for regret. In the early years of mass consumption, many people moved from no choice to choice. No cars to a toss-up between the Ford, Honda, or Buick. The initial uncertainty produced anxiety. But when people get used to choice, anxiety disappears. Limited choice generates anxiety, infinite choice breeds indifference.

There are more paradoxes than straight lines. No longer racked by guilt or tortured by choice, the affluent postmoderns can get on with the pursuit of happiness, self-fulfillment, and personal growth. But they don't. Not all of them. Ecological awareness, social conscience, sensitivity, and compassion have not disappeared. The paradoxes are even richer: despite the pessimism Beckett was a comic writer, there was humor in anxiety; Disney was an unhappy man always seeing Communists at work, and I can think of no more joyless occasion than my own visit to Disneyland. It is only half-right to say that Disney has replaced Beckett as an icon, and enjoyment has displaced suffering as fashionable attitudes. It is also half-wrong. Such is the pleasure of paradox.

Architecture (Postmodern)

Buildings lock up history; they provide a solid testimony to shifting fashions, a concrete record of changing styles. Postmodern architecture was a reaction to modernist architecture, which, in theory, was a style that stressed simplicity, honesty to materials, and an explicit link between form and function. In practice, it meant flat-topped, box-looking tower blocks sheathed in concrete and glass that were built all over the world in exactly the same style. Communist headquarters in Warsaw, corporate offices in New York, government buildings in Rio de Janeiro and Lagos, public housing in Chicago and London all looked the same—all had the simple, clean lines, the box look, and the flat top. Now you can understand its other name, the International style. This was the concrete metanarrative of modernism.

Commentators began to sense something was happening when one of the archpriests of modernist architecture, the American Philip Johnson (1906–), designed the AT&T Building in New York. The building, which opened in 1978, had, rather than the usual flat top, a pediment that looked like the top of a Chippendale highboy. To the architects and architectural commentators, this was a big deal. This was the same Philip Johnson who had cowritten *The International Style* (1932), who had built his own house in New Canaan, Connecticut, in 1949 as an uncompromising and austere glass box, and who had designed the Seagram Building (1958) in New York with the modernist guru Mies van der Rohe. Now, the same Philip Johnson was adding ornamentation to a prestige building. This was just a taste of things to come. Ornamentation was in, historical referencing was in. The result was apartment buildings with Corinthian towers, post offices as Greek temples, office buildings with Georgian façades, museums with Renaissance decoration. Arches were in, pediments and columns were in, color was in. The result was an architecture that was fun, colorful, sometimes tacky, often repetitive, with a capacity to annoy and humor. Architectural integrity now meant quoting the past as well as indicating the future. Architecture that could provoke a smile. In the riot of subsequent color and whimsy, the AT&T Building began to change from a revolutionary statement to a model of understatement and austere good taste.

Modernist architecture had a theory of liberation. Drawing

ideological sustenance from the Bauhaus school, it extolled, in theory if not in practice, the belief that architecture was liberating, the built form of a new social order. Postmodern architecture has lost that sense of ideological purpose. Emancipatory doctrines of the built environment have had such a bad press that we now lack faith in the ability of our cities to liberate us. A new form of bunker architecture has been developed in which the rich live behind fortified hiding places and "public" buildings are designed to keep out the street people. New hotels do not have easy pedestrian access, and airport seats are designed so that you cannot lie down. Security and surveillance have become part of the syntax of postmodern architecture as much as whimsy and historicism have.

Postmodern architecture is an architecture that looks forward to the past; it reflects the decline of the metanarrative of modernist confidence and condenses the hopes and anxieties of the contemporary, an edgy humor atop a shaky foundation.

Authenticity

In 1927 the Russian filmmaker Sergei Eisenstein (1898–1948) made *October*. The climax of the film is the storming of the Winter Palace. Crowds build up in the streets outside the wall. Eventually, the weight of numbers and the force of collective anger sweep through the gates and up the stairs. The palace guards are eventually routed and, in a hugely symbolic scene, statues are destroyed. The old order is toppled.

The scene comes straight from Eisenstein's imagination. There was no storming of the Winter Palace even remotely like that portrayed on the screen. More people died in the making of the film than the "real" takeover of the palace. Scenes from the movie are often used in many documentaries of the Russian Revolution. They are still used, sometimes with quotation marks around them, often not. The images that came from Eisenstein's imaginative reconstructions of real events became the events themselves.

The mixing of fact with fancy, reality with illusion has undermined our notion of the real. Even the term *real* should have permanent quotation marks wreathed around it as a constant reminder of the quixotic nature of reality in the postmodern world.

We carry around pictures of the world in our heads. These may come from direct experience with the outside world, the world outside of our heads. But in a world of images, the world we now inhabit, more of these pictures come not from direct contact with the "real" world but mediated through the reconstructions of film, advertisements, television, jingles, videos. Eisenstein's storming has become the "real" storming of the Winter Palace.

The concern for authenticity has changed our language. "Do you mean it?" has been replaced by "Do you really mean it?" The fear of inauthenticity has inflated the currency of our communication. We need more coinage of qualification and exaggeration. One of the most effective advertising slogans is "It's the Real Thing."

Comparing the underlying real with the apparent reality was one modernist solution. It was not the only one, there was also a creative concern with the nature of representation, hence surrealism and cubism. But a dominant element was getting to the bottom of things, finding the underlying structure, ripping away at the mask of everyday reality to find a deeper, transcendent reality. These were part of the modernist search for knowledge. They are still part of many people's lives. The search for that authentic holiday in the Dordogne or getting a "real" Italian meal are problems that continue to plague the intelligentsia ever eager to distance themselves from the masses. The other solution is to give up the search for the Holy Grail of the "real." Not only accept the blurring, revel in it. Don't mock the phoniness of Disneyland, see it as another reality. Accept and explore the multiplicity of realities. After all, if its "real" for some people, it must be real. The multiplicity of realities creates confusion, excitement, and hope. We can become confused if the multiple realities contradict our view of the world. Did people land on the moon, or was it a hoax? Are there many gods? The retreat to fundamentalism is one response to the anxiety of uncertainty. The uncertainty can also cause excitement, the kaleidoscope roller coaster of living in many possible realities. Living in the same place, we can connect with so many different communities, each with its own reality that our view of the world can easily change. For some, the possibility of changing their reality provides hope. The growth of self-help counseling and books is one indication of the belief that our present lives are only one "reality." Unsuccessful in work? Try positive thinking or creative imaging to release the real you, the you you always wanted to become. "Reality" is no longer a fixed category; it has become a set of infinite possibilities.

Author

The author used to be the person who wrote the book. In the postmodernist world, the author has been declared dead. Long live the creative reader.

In the act of reading or seeing or in other interpretative acts, the creator's role used to be seen as central. But that assumes a simple transmission of the author's intentions to the readers' interpretation. A hierarchy was assumed between the creative author and the passive, consuming reader. The death of the author comes from the notion that the author is not the only creative force at work. The reader too has a creative role.

The creative reader can be seen in the multiple readings of an author's work. Jane Austen (1775–1817) has been seen as an amusing chronicler of the English landed gentry, an apologist for a corrupt, class-based society, or an early feminist writer whose concentration on the domestic sphere is a sensitive portrayal of woman's role in a patriarchal society. You pays your money and you takes your choice. Each reading is possible, but it all depends on the reader.

The notion of a creative reader undermines the concept of a hierarchy of culture. There are no longer great authors, only some authors who have more creative readers than others. And if we have creative readers, then even poor-quality work can be redeemed by a high-quality reading. Authors or even whole genres, such as the cowboy western novel, previously dismissed as trashy, have been reclaimed.

Individual authors go into and out of fashion. Jane Austen is more popular now than at any time in the past one hundred years. The changing fashions tell us much about our postmodern world. The work of female authors, working-class authors, writers from minority groups, oppressed cultures, or marginalized societies is now being seen as more important and more valuable.

One paradox of the creative-reader debate has always fascinated me. Why do the people who write about the death of the author always have their name prominently displayed?

Baldness

Remember when Yul Brynner was the only famous person who was bald? At least the only person who cultivated his baldness.

Now baldness is in. Michel Foucault, Michael Jordan, Sinead O'Connor . . . the list goes on. The new man can feel comfortable with his baldness. For women it shows a lack of concern with stereotypical feminine identity. Being bald is no longer something to be ashamed of. For the more daring, it is a look to be achieved, cultivated, marketed. Baldness and charisma—the new combination for both men and women. There are still some who cling to the old discourse of hair equals charisma. Hair denial is still apparent in those men who wrap their few remaining strands around their head in a desperate attempt to hide the glistening pate, while wigs are still a much-used part of the wardrobe of many famous film actors and television personalities. But these are the residuals. Baldness is celebrated rather than denied. Bald is beautiful.

Beach

A beach is an area of half-land, half-sea where the sea meets the land. Beaches used to be quite lonely places, inhabited by the occasional fishers, migratory wildlife, and partying teenagers hungry for outdoor sex. From the latter half of the nineteenth century, and particularly in the past thirty years, the beach has become the icon of the hedonist lifestyle, the place of body display, the setting for the sensual. The beach has become playground for children and adults alike.

When most people worked outdoors, the tanned, weather-beaten look was common. It indicated manual labor. The rich wanted to distinguish themselves by looking as if they spent most of their time indoors. But when more people started working in factories and offices, the pale complexion became the mark of the working classes and the tanned look became the desired body decoration for the rich. The style percolated down the social hierarchy. Lying on the beach and getting a tan is now one of the most popular outdoor leisure pursuits. And the result is the growth of a beach culture and even beach cities. The whole orientation of urban form has been altered. New cities now hug the coast, and some of the most rapidly growing cities are along the coast. If you fly into Miami, Florida, you can see how the new Sunbelt cities elongate themselves along the coast to maximize beach frontage. More than ever before, cities and people are facing the sea.

With the destruction of the ozone level and the consequent dangers of greater risk of skin cancer with exposure to the sun, the fashion for suntanned bodies may be either replaced by a return to the fragile look or simulated with paint-on tans. Will beaches then resort back to the fisherman?

Biodegradable

Biodegradable is an environmentally acceptable form of consumption; it gives an air of naturalness, a down-home earthiness to all kinds of products. "Natural" materials and biodegradable products all suggest a harmony between human production and consumption, and the so-called natural world.

Things are defined by their opposite. The polarity to biodegradable is synthetic. Plastic was one of the great creations of modernity, the application of science to create an organic material that did not wear out. It was a mythic product, a human creation not subject to the weathering of time and use. Plastic was the product of the modern period. These same properties make it undesirable in the postmodern age. "That's plastic" is now a form of abuse, a pointed criticism that suggests phoniness, not natural. Plastic things are not biodegradable but are half-redeemable if they are "recyclable." If they do not waste away, at least they can be reused.

The lauding of natural implied by the term biodegradable marks the reversing of the CULTURE-nature structure of modernity to the NATURE-culture patterning of postmodernity. Both the modernist capitalists and socialists shared a vision of nature brought under control, harnessed, and conquered. The construction of cities, the manufacturing of commodities, the building of human communities—these were the mark of progress and civilization. For the postmoderns nature is to be protected as well as used. Sustainable development, ecological diversity—these are the postmodern catchwords, while the symbols of civilization now include the saving of the rainforest and the protection of the environment.

Body

The mind was the principal organ in the modern world. The body fulfills that role in the postmodern age. "I think therefore I am" was the motto of the Age of Reason from the Enlightenment to the near present; it was also, according to the postmodern novelist Milan Kundera, the voice of the intellectual who underestimated the pain of toothache. Feeling has replaced thinking as the dominant mode of experience and description. "How do you feel?" has almost replaced "What do you think?" as the most-used question in social interaction. It is our bodies that make us individuals, not our minds; feeling, not rationality; sensuality, not analysis. The cult of the body beautiful now vies with the cultivation of the mind. The corporeal is winning against the cerebral as the dominant mode of experience and expression. From the exploration of the body in greater sexual awareness to the celebration of the body in the explosion of various outdoor activities and the maintenance of a "healthy" look, from the rise of beach cities to the emphasis on looking young, the body is winning out against the mind. It was Woody Allen who wrote that the brain is the most overrated organ. "I feel therefore I am" is the new motto.

Capitalism

Things are defined by their opposite. At its birth capitalism was the upstart competitor to feudalism. It replaced a moral economy with a money economy. Later, it was defined in opposition to socialism, and the operation of the free market was extolled against the rigidities of the planned economy. Capitalism has stood the test of time; history has validated capitalism as feudalism; and, more recently, socialism has receded into historical irrelevancy.

Adam Smith's *Wealth of Nations* was published in 1776. In the same year came the American Declaration of Independence. The rise of capitalism and the United States have gone hand in hand. There is a parallel and a linkage. The end of the cold war was important for both. For both the United States and the supporters of capitalism, this was not so much a victory as the beginning of a period of introspective self-doubt. Capitalism had won. There was now no longer any need to justify the free market. The question became not a choice between capitalism or socialism but what kind of capitalism. Critics pointed to the environmental costs of sustained economic growth and the continued inequalities at the national and international levels, while more fundamental criticisms pointed to the lack of connection between economic growth and human happiness.

Rather than speak of capitalism in the singular, it is more appropriate to consider capitalisms. The mode of production varies around the world. In some places it is associated with high wages and liberal democracies; in others it goes hand in hand with naked exploitation and repressive political regimes. Capitalism is a chameleon. That is its strength. It has outlasted its more rigid competitors.

One of the biggest changes of recent years has been referred to as post-Fordism. Let's back up a bit. In 1903 Henry Ford (1863–1947) founded the Ford Motor Company. His intention was to make a car "so low in price that no man making a good salary will be unable to own one." He proved true to his words. In 1908 the first Model T rolled off the production line, and by 1927, 15 million of them had been sold. Fordism, as a generic name, was associated with mass production, the techniques of the assembly line, the creation of low-cost consumption goods for a mass market. Fordism was the capitalist system of assembly-line manufacture that resulted in high productivity and high wages. In 1914 Ford paid his workers $5 a day, an unheard of amount for the time.

There is a more technical use of the term. Fordism was the name given to the mass production of commodities on controlled assembly lines, an inflexible assembly line geared toward the constant production of a standardized commodity. You could buy the Model T Ford in any color as long as it was black. Post-Fordism involves greater flexibility of production of an increasing range of products with shorter runs. This implies more subcontracting, greater vertical integration between firms, and a more "flexible" use of labor. Flexible production is the response of capital to a tighter market, the declining power of organized labor, and rapid shifts in consumer preferences. Flexible production enables firms to adjust quickly to a more volatile market, allows high rates of productivity growth, and reduces employment costs. Flexible production involves a change in the relationship between labor and capital; in effect it gives capital greater control over the deployment of labor, the pacing of work, and the costs of labor. Fordism implied high-paying, secure employment, conditions that allowed labor organizations to flourish and increase in strength. Post-Fordist techniques both reflect and condense the weaker position of the workforce. An increasing bifurcation has been noted between a core of highly paid, trained employees with good working conditions and generous benefits and an increasing number of more peripheral workers employed part-time on a more irregular basis with fewer benefits or advancement opportunities.

Capitalism has proved to be one of the most resilient and adaptable economic systems. The question is whether the evolution can continue to produce a fairer, more environmentally friendly system that can meet emotional as well as material needs, fill hungry mouths as well as aching hearts. Capitalism is no longer compared to feudalism or socialism—it is now used to carry the full load of human expectations. That is a heavy burden.

Cohort

The initial definition of *cohort* is the tenth part of a Roman legion. Its use has widened to include any group of the same age.

Your life is a function of where you are. Most of us know that life in the affluent suburbs of the United States is very different than that in the slums of Rio or the desiccated plains of Africa. Less obvious is the variation over time. Your experience of life is also a function of when you are.

An example. In 1964 the Australian writer Donald Horne wrote a book entitled *The Lucky Country*. It was and still is widely believed in that country that the title accurately reflected the blessed nature of the country, a place endowed with a sunny climate, an easy lifestyle, and a society unmarred by the strife and violence common in other parts of the world. That the book did not praise Australia is now beside the point; the title, like the misreading, became part of the self-definition of the country.

The book was first published in 1964, revised in 1968, and

given the designation of Australian classic by the publisher Angus and Robertson in 1978. The book was conceived, written, and consumed very largely in a period of rising affluence in both Australia and around the world. Other countries were too old to forge a cultural identity based on a sudden upsurge of widespread affluence. Australia was not. Almost two hundred years of boat people had always been eager to justify their decision and praise their destination. Recent migrants joined with home-grown nationalists in believing the adjective of Horne's title. The temporary, worldwide phenomenon of increasing affluence was thus eagerly appropriated as a peculiarly Australian condition. But the condition was not simply a function of space. It was not Australia, but Australia of that time. It was not so much the Lucky Country as the Lucky Cohort. If you were born into the middle classes from 1940 to 1950, you avoided the Great Depression and were coming onto the job market in the 1950s and 1960s, when unemployment was less than 1 percent. Born in 1940 and trained as an academic, you are now a professor despite your dismal publishing record. Interested in law you are a senior barrister, maybe even a judge. Keen on politics you probably have a comfortable sinecure with the New South Wales public service. Even with more modest aims, you still purchased a cheap house with low-interest loans, and you have a job history of continuous employment and rising income. In much of the rich world, the Lucky Cohort had most of the benefits and few of the sacrifices. An older generation had the depression and the war. A younger generation had failing economies and restricted opportunities. People of similar status but different ages have very different experiences. Young academics, for example, have limited opportunities, their fate decided by full professors with perhaps a record of mediocrity but with the advantage of being born at the right time. Our lives are a reflection not simply of where we are in the world and in our respective communities but when we are. Who we are is a function of time as well as space.

Cold War

Remember the cold war? It was the division of the world into two opposing camps headed by the Soviet Union and the United States. For forty-five years, from 1945 until 1990, the globe was riven by this central fracture. The system was kept in a state of dynamic instability, underwritten by one of the most appropriate acronyms, mutually assured destruction, MAD. The security of the world rested on the bizarre proposition that either side was ready to bomb the whole planet back to the Stone Age. Well, now that the cold war is over, the results can be declared: the losers were the Soviet Union and the United States; the winners were Japan and Germany.

The Soviet Union bankrupted itself by trying to keep up with the arms race, by going after high-profile, prestige projects like putting people in space while at home the system had trouble feeding its people; and when it did feed the people it did not have their loyalty or respect. There was a crisis of legitimation that came to a head in the late 1980s. The Soviet Union collapsed from the inside, like a house of cards eventually toppled by its own insecure foundations. The "new" state of the Soviet Union fractured along the "old" ethnic and cultural divisions that predated the Bolshevik Revolution.

But didn't the United States win the cold war? Well yes and no. The United States won, if you mean by winning that it defeated its enemy. The Soviet Union was involved in an arms race that eventually bankrupted the system. The United States also lost. To win meant that it created a huge military-industrial complex that lay at the heart of the US economy and the US view of itself. The military buildup distorted the US economy, which could produce hypersophisticated missiles for a shrinking market but could not make a successful car for the world market. Research and development was concentrated into military activities. Who buys a video, television, or camcorder made in the United States? Victory in the cold war meant economic defeat in the marketplaces of the world.

The conflict with the Soviet Union was the central defining characteristic for the United States. It was like a western: there were guys with white hats against guys with black hats, it was us against them, good against evil. Whole generations of politicians and political analysts and whole organizations such as the Pentagon, CIA, and FBI could only understand the world through this prism. It was a simple but all-encompassing view of the world that delayed domestic improvements and reform. A national health system could not be introduced because it smacked of communism; the same with education, housing, and transport. Self-imposed limitations restricted domestic reform and social improvements.

The real victors of the cold war were Japan and Germany. Defeated in the Second World War, their societies and economies were completely restructured. A generation grew up committed to hard work and economic growth. Limitations were placed on their military spending, which meant they could allocate resources, talent, and drive to competing in the expanding markets of the world economy. They did not have to spend money on defense because their defense was provided by the United States. Without an evil Other to define themselves or to restrict their development and without the burden of a "world" role, they could get on with the business of making and selling goods that people wanted.

Commodification

At the end of the US football championship, the Superbowl, a player is awarded the status of MVP, most valuable player. It is a highly coveted honor. MVP status is also awarded after basketball and baseball championships. There is no award for best player, the most sportsmanlike player, or even the best loved player. The award is simply for the most valuable.

Commodification refers to the process whereby things become more and more valued in monetary terms. Take the case of shelter. In the distant past, we built our own house, and it had value as something to keep us safe from the elements. This is use value. When we own our dwellings they still have use value as a source of shelter, but they also have exchange value—they can be bought and sold, they can be a source of wealth and income. Housing, like athletic prowess, has become commodified. When things previously valued for their use value take on exchange value, we can speak of the process of commodification. Capitalism and commodification go hand in hand. In the postmodern world, however, commodification has been extended into new realms, into the world of experiences, relationships, and feelings. In the late nineteenth century, savvy capitalists made commodities like iron and steel. In the late twentieth century, the smart capitalists sell us experiences in theme parks, provide us with conversation and company in expensive psychoanalysis courses, make us feel happy or sad or just plain scared at the movies. Not only are things sold but images are as well. A pair of jeans becomes twice as expensive with the addition of a designer name. People's names become commodities. Chanel. Pierre Cardin. Ralph Lauren. We buy not only their things but their name, their view of the world. Even human relationships have become commodified. The sons, daughters, former husbands and wives of famous people sell their "story" to magazines and publishers. Personal experiences turned into marketable stories. Use value into exchange value. Experience into money. Feelings into bank accounts. The extension of commodification into what was once the most private and the most personal.

Decolonization

One of the great transformations of the modern period was the colonization of most of the world by European powers: Portugal and Spain in the sixteenth and seventeenth centuries, then England, Holland, and France in the seventeenth and eighteenth centuries. In the first three-quarters of the nineteenth century, Britain reigned supreme, until there was another grab for territory by the United States, Germany, Belgium, and France. The world had a definite shape. It was controlled by a small number of industrial countries eager to obtain territory for economic reasons, to stop their competitors from gaining an advantage, and for reasons of prestige. Why else would tiny Belgium grab such a huge chunk of central Africa?

Colonization and imperialism left little of the world untouched by their presence and their cultural fallout. The culture of Western Europe became the standard, the reference point to compare others to, and the zenith to be obtained in the forward march of history.

Decolonization was one of the most important social movements of the post–Second World War era. In the late 1940s, Britain's Asian empire began to fall: India, Pakistan, Sri Lanka, and Burma. Indonesia became independent from The Netherlands. Through the 1950s and 1960s, much of Asia and most of Africa overturned the formal imperial bonds. Political independence was achieved much more easily than economic independence. The economies of the newly independent states are still controlled by and connected to the rich core of the world economy. Wealth is very unevenly spread, and poverty and poor health are endemic conditions for the majority of the population.

Decolonization was and still is a cultural movement. Colonization stressed the superiority of European culture. Decolonization stresses the Othering of non- European culture. There is a vibrant school of postcolonial criticism that celebrates the diversity of cultures that make up the world and systematically criticizes the intentions and consequences of European expansionism. Decolonization is an angle of vision, a cultural endeavor that seeks to rescue non-European cultures from insignificance. It would even dispute the term *non-European*, implying as it does one cultural standard. The postcolonial world has its emphasis on cultural diversity, cultural resistance, and the struggle to escape universal norms.

Deconstructionism

This is a translation from the French term *deconstruction*, meaning to take apart. It is most commonly associated with the work of the French philosopher Jacques Derrida (1931–). Derrida is concerned with constructing a strategy to expose the metaphysical assumptions that lie behind the last two thousand years of philosophical writing. Derrida's argument is that all of this writing is founded on a desire for certainty, for some fundamental source of meaning. He identified this trait even in such modernist philosophers as Heidegger and Nietzsche. Derrida's claim is that we should resist such desires.

To his critics Derrida is against reason. His taking apart involves a fundamental assault. It is the destruction of the house of reason first laid down by the Enlightenment, leaving behind bombed-out remains smoldering on an existential plain.

To his supporters Derrida disrupts the cozy assumptions of

philosophy. His strategy of deconstructionism is a radical, subversive reading of texts that unearths all the taken-for-granted assumptions. Deconstructionism involves a questioning of all the moral and political principles that have guided Western civilization. It is the Othering of philosophy and the philosophy of the Other.

Derrida is one member of that small though powerful group of French intellectuals who have influenced cultural thought and criticism in the past fifty years. Others include Althusser, Barthes, Foucault, Sartre, and Baudrillard. Derrida's reception is somewhat typical of French academic superstars. Born in Algiers and educated in Paris, Derrida followed a rigorous academic program. His first book, published in 1962, was a study of the philosopher Edmund Husserl. His three big books were *Speech and Phenomena* (1967; trans. 1973), *Writing and Difference* (1967; trans. 1978), and *Of Grammatology* (1967; trans. 1976). Throughout the 1980s his name diffused from a narrow range of philosophers to a much broader academic audience. He became one of the charmed names of the intelligentsia used by critics of postmodernism as an example of antireason and the irrational, empty reading of texts. For the cheerleaders of postmodernism, he lead the charge against modernism, and his strategy of deconstructionism was a powerful blowtorch to the accumulated modernist dogma.

Discourse

Discourse is an oft-used word. A simple definition: a framework that includes whole sets of ideas, words, concepts, and practices. Discourses are the general context in which ideas take on a specific meaning and inform particular practices. An example: the term *family* is employed in different ways in different discourses.

In the technical sociological literature, it refers to a group of blood relations living together, subdefinitions include nuclear family and extended family. In the rhetoric of politics, however, the term *family* is used to appeal to a whole set of values, beliefs, narratives. When conservative politicians speak of the decline of family values, the word *family* is like a land mine set to explode a whole shrapnel of emotions, prejudices, and beliefs. Same word but very different meanings in the two discourses.

The term is closely linked to two other ideas. The term *paradigm* was first used by the philosopher of science T. S. Kuhn (1922–) to refer to a conceptual schema that defines both the objects and the methods of investigation. The normal work of natural scientists takes places within the guidelines of one paradigm, but as anomalies and unexplained facts are encountered, the stage is set for a revolutionary upheaval in which a new and better paradigm is fashioned. This is what happened in the shift from the mechanical world of Newtonian physics to the relativity of Einsteinian physics. The new paradigm then provides the guidelines for a new round of scientific endeavor until this paradigm, in turn, is faced with unexplained and unexplainable facts. Paradigms, like discourses, set new questions as well provide new answers. What was considered important in one paradigm is considered insignificant in another.

The term *problematic* was used by the French philosopher Louis Althusser (1918–) to refer to systems of concepts that define both the problems set for intellectual endeavor and the means to provide and verify the answers. Althusser's work was concerned primarily with justifying the historical materialism of Marxism as a science and with his careful "reading" of Marx.

One of Althusser's students at the Ecole Normale Supérieure in Paris was the historian Michel Foucault (1926–84). The term *discourse* is most often associated with Foucault. All postmoderns have heard of Foucault. Some have even read him. Foucault was an original thinker. In a series of books, he studied the discourses and practices of power, not the general notion of power but power wielded in specific places by particular people against certain, categorized people. He studied the discourses and practices that defined madness, illness, punishment, and sexuality. His books include *Madness and Civilization* (1961), *The Archaeology of Knowledge* (1972), *The Birth of the Clinic* (1973), and *The History of Sexuality* (1976–83). Like James Dean and Elvis Presley, a relatively early death gave his work a cachet that longevity may have denied.

Disneyland

In 1953 at a convention of amusement park owners, a successful film animator presented plans for a new park. The savvy owners knew it was going to be a failure. There was too much open space and not enough revenue-generating rides. The whole idea was doomed to economic ruin. Two years later the park opened in Orange County, just south of Los Angeles. It was called Disneyland.

Disneyland, and the later Disneyworld of Florida and the Euro-Disney that opened in 1992 outside of Paris, help to define postmodernity. They are more than just amusement parks. They are about the careful re-creation of a past that never existed, a guided narrative round the imagined past, the unreal present, and the nostalgic future. By the time you read this book, almost 40 million people will have been to Disneyland, wandered down Main Street, and taken a ride in the ninth largest submarine fleet in the world. Disneyland collapses the distinction between the authentic and the unreal, the past and the present, the politics of pleasure and the pleasure of education. My own visit in 1985 was anticlimactic. Disneyland has become such a figure of speech, a metaphor, and an icon for me that the "reality" (and I use the word advisedly) of the place can never match up to the expectation.

Disneyland is one of the earliest in a long line of theme parks. This is the narration of pleasure, the management of delight, the organization of enjoyment. Authenticity is self-referenced and not necessarily anchored to the external world, as in the sixteenth-century English village in Upstate New York, the nineteenth-century New England whaling port in San Diego, California, or the medieval banqueting hall in suburban Nottingham. They are exact copies of things that never existed, sites of hyperreality and as redolent of their times as Gothic cathedrals, Renaissance palaces, or modernist skyscrapers. Four miles from where I live in the rural landscape of Upstate New York is a sign that advertises Ye Olde Pizza Pub. When I no longer found this sign strange, ambiguous, or paradoxical, I knew that I was on my way to becoming a postmodern.

Enlightenment

The Enlightenment is the name given to a myriad group of trends gestating in Europe in the seventeenth century and coming to fruition in the middle of the eighteenth. The early trends are associated with such names as Bacon and Descartes, Spinoza and Locke. Later writers include Fontenelle, Voltaire, Rousseau, Hume, Kant, and Adam Smith. Among the many ideas of the Enlightenment, let me mention just three notions: that the natural world can be understood through rational critical thought; that scientific method can be applied to the social world as well as to the natural world; that the application of reason can lead to material and social progress.

At the heart of the Enlightenment is the concept of reason and the belief that the application of reason can solve problems. Even the term *Enlightenment* conjures up images of light being brought to darkness, the glow of reason and rationality brightening up a shadowy world of prejudice and opinion. In the modernist conception, the Enlightenment was a Good Thing, a precursor of the modern world, a source of progress. One of the defining elements of postmodernity is the questioning of this cozy assumption. The subjection of the natural world to a scientific rationality has, according to some, been the cause of tremendous environmental damage as a soulless science replaced a more organic connection with the earth. The scientific method applied to society may have produced better government policies, but it was also the incubator of fascism. Some critics of the Enlightenment draw a line from the eighteenth-century salons of Paris to the concentration camps of Germany. In the Enlightenment postmodern critics see the origin of many of our contemporary ills: the rupturing of facts and values, the separation of scientific method from social concerns, and the dissolution of the connection between people and the environment.

At the heart of the postmodern critique is the gnawing feeling that progress is not all that it was cracked up to be. If the trajectory is seen as downward rather than upward, then the Enlightenment becomes the source of the Fall rather than the starting point for progress.

The Enlightenment conjures up images of men in book-lined studies, shelves full of the writings of classical authors. Feminist critique, postcolonial criticism, and a new sexual politics all dispute the claim to universality of this perspective. Postmodernism "otherizes" Enlightenment Man.

Environment

The globalizing discourse at the heart of postmodernity is the environment. This is a loose concept. The looseness is appropriate, for it allows the notion to be wrapped around a whole variety of different flagpoles. Environment is caring for the earth, saving the whale, protecting the rainforest, cleaning up pollution, creating sustainable development. Like all myths it has good guys and bad guys and an epic venture. The bad guys are the polluters, men who club seals, destroy rain forests, dump toxic wastes into pristine rivers. The epic quest is the need and desire to turn culture back into nature, the settled into the wild, the defiled into the pure, the profane into the sacred.

The environment as an idea is broad enough and deep enough to capture the global imagination and create the basis for a global discourse. In the post–cold war world, it is one of the ventures that has the capacity to generate enthusiasm, stimulate action, and still allow people to feel good.

No one is against the environment. In a time of supposed resistance to totalizing discourse, is it a paradox that the environment is just that?

Family

Industrialization and urbanization severed the links of the extended family. The nuclear family was one of the creations of modernity. The nuclear family became the dominant cultural image of family life. Mom, Dad and the two kids, with Mom at home and Dad at work, became the family icon. Its zenith was in the 1950s and 1960s, especially in the richest countries, particularly in the United States. The move to the suburban house became the mythic destination of the US family in the 1960s just as the move west was the destination of the 1860s. The image was reinforced by the consumer-orientated industries eager to find a peg on which to hang their advertising campaigns.

A paradox. The nuclear family became more important in political rhetoric just as it was disappearing in empirical importance. In the United States, for example, the total number of married couples with children as a percentage of all households has shrunk from 40 percent in 1970 to 25 percent in 1992. More than one in every four households in the United States are single-parent households; half of all marriages end in divorce; births to single mothers constitute one in four of all births. The nuclear family is declining because more people are living on their own, more married people are not having children, and more people who are having children are not married. Even within the nuclear family the image of woman at home is fast disappearing as women express their desire and need to work. The suburban lifestyle of the 1960s can be maintained in the 1990s only with two wage earners.

The rhetoric, however, sees the decline as a function not of economic but of moral decay. In this perspective the family is the source of moral stability and integrity. (Incest, child abuse, and neglect notwithstanding). The demand for a return to "family values," whatever they are, is a pointer not to a return but to a leave-taking. The rhetoric is a nostalgic commitment to something that has lost its empirical and cultural dominance.

Feminism

Feminism has been one of the most important elements in the new climate of opinion that some have labeled as postmodern. Feminism subverts the modernist conceptions of class with gender, replaces politics with sexual politics, and disputes the convenient demarcation of the private and the domestic from the public and the political.

Feminism has some deep roots. In 1792 Mary Wollstonecraft's *Vindication of the Rights of Women* was published. Throughout the nineteenth century and into the twentieth, people campaigned for women's suffrage. Although the success gave women the vote, it did not give them political power. A more recent feminist discourse sought a realignment of the world: the replacement of history with herstory, the identification of sexist practices in institutions, the struggle to liberate women from stereotyping. The politics of liberation demand more child care facilities, equal pay for equal work, and changes in laws regarding marriage, property, and birth control. The struggle has been successful at a variety of levels. Sexism is now seen as politically incorrect. There has been a large change in attitudes over a short period of time that is truly remarkable. Inequalities still exist; and while some point to the successes, some indicate the length of the journey still to be undertaken. Feminism, like a torrent braiding into different streams, has split into a variety of (dis)courses. There are some feminists who see men as the problem, some who see patriarchy as the problem, and some who see capitalism as the problem. There has also been the appearance of iconoclastic postfeminists, some who see women themselves as part of the problem, and some who do not see a problem.

Feminism has contributed to postmodernism. It has also been subverted by postmodernism. If there is no metanarrative, no one big story of gender, then the male-female dichotomy is only one of a whole variety of differences; rich/poor, black/white, straight/gay, young/old. Feminism has placed gender issues onto the agenda, but other sources of difference are demanding attention. Much of the feminist political rhetoric of the 1970s and early 1980s expressed the concerns of white, straight, affluent women in the richer countries of the world. The voices of black women, gay women, poor women, and women in the Third World are combining feminism with issues and practices of race, sexuality, wealth, and cultural identity. Postfeminism will enhance and contest postmodernism.

Film

Although there were important developments in film in the nineteenth century, film as both art form and mass entertainment is at one and the same time a product and a record of the twentieth century. The first film theater was built in Pittsburgh, Pennsylvania, in 1905, and from then until now film has captured, reflected, distorted, heightened, condensed, promoted, and created the dreams, beliefs, ideas, values, and experiences of the masses. From the early, soundless, flickering pictures to the multimillion dollar specials of today, films have provided the folktales, heroes, and villains of the contemporary world. Film is the most important form of mass entertainment.

Films are consumed globally but are produced on mass scale in just a few places. The Indian cinema has an enormous following and the European movie industry waxes and wanes, but the most enduring site is Hollywood. One result is that specifically US concerns are given a privileged cinematic position; and yet the need for global audiences means that much of the specificities of US history and society are ignored. It is the United States of the global imagination that is predominantly portrayed by Hollywood.

The film industry has survived many changes: the decline of the studio system, the rise of television, and the growing use of video recorders at the expense of the box office. The first change affected the form of production. The latter two affected the form of consumption. But all three together have not undermined the basic cinematic form of a ninety-minute to two-hour "story." The most modern of artistic forms is set to become one of the most enduring.

The dominance of film consumption has affected the way we all look at the world. The use of montage, dissolved-time sequences, the running of several story lines in parallel, and the nonlinear form of storytelling have fractured the predominant linear narratives of pre-film forms. The contemporary novel, for example, now owes its form as much to movies as to previous literature. Its supercondensed form is the rock video, at its best a three-minute exercise in advanced film technique. Film started off as a means of entertainment; it has become a lens of perception. Films provide us with an opportunity to "see" other lives, other places, other times. They are one of our main sources of collective myth and group fantasy, global education and shared knowledge. Films let us see how similar we are and how different.

Gender

The identification of gender as a social rather than a biological issue has been one of the most significant developments of recent years. Gender has been reclaimed from biology. For most of the postwar period up to the 1970s, social debates and even language were not so much blind to gender differences as simply seeing gender roles as fixed, eternal creations of biological difference. It was chairman, spokesman, man and environment, man and the modern world. Behind the words lay a belief and a practice that had marginalized many women to the domestic sphere, to child-rearing, the home, and the hearth. There were important differences by class and race. Poorer women and women of color often had to work outside the home. The image of the mother at home was strongest in the middle- and upper-income categories of the rich world.

Two movements have altered the way we see gender. The first has been the feminist critique. One important strand has argued that biological differences need not and should not imply or involve differential power, limited access to employment, or restricted social and political opportunities. More recently, an emerging men's movement has argued that the traditional gender divisions hurt men as well as women. The traditional gender divisions distort the full development of men as well as women. Men get the feeling of power, women get the power of feeling; both lose something in the process. Gender is now much more a political than a biological issue. As much individual choice as social categorization.

The particular postmodern twist to this debate is to focus on the arbitrary nature of the division and to bring the shadowy borderlands into a brighter light. The focus on androgyny, the increasing influence of cross-dressing on fashion, the popularity of such pop stars as Michael Jackson and movies like *The Crying Game* all highlight the cultural possibilities as well as the social anxieties of genderbending, gender ambiguities, and gender uncertainty. People are divided by their gender into women and men. This division is not innocent. And in the postmodern world the division is neither fixed and secure nor an unchanging basis for personal and group identity.

Glasgow

The city of Glasgow on the banks of the River Clyde in Scotland is a point of intersection for two important trends—deindustrialization and the selling of places.

The name of the city derives from the Celtic *Glasghu*, which can be translated as beloved green spot. Its first surge of growth came after the Treaty of Union between England and Scotland in 1707. The treaty allowed Glasgow to trade with the colonies of the West Indies and North America. Like the other west coast ports of Liverpool and Bristol, Glasgow did well from this trade, particularly with the import of tobacco. In 1768 the Clyde was deepened, allowing ships to come further up the estuary and dock in the center of the city. Glasgow became a rich mercantile city where wealthy merchants displayed their affluence. Visitors to Glasgow in the eighteenth and very early nineteenth centuries all commented on the beauty of the city. In 1730 Edward Burt described it as "the prettiest and most uniform Town that I ever saw"; and even as late as 1771, the novelist Tobias Smollett could see it as "one of the prettiest towns in Europe."

From the late eighteenth century, Glasgow became one of the epicenters of the industrial revolution. In 1799 bleaching powder was patented in the city, and in 1822 the first blast furnace was put into operation. The city was transformed by the new economic order. Shipbuilding, iron and steel production, the manufacture of locomotives, chemical works, printing and dyeing, whisky blending and bottling, flour milling, and engineering. The city developed an international market for its products. The growth of the city was dramatic. Between 1780 and 1830, the population of the city increased fivefold. Yet the urban fabric remained the same. The effects were huge population densities and the overwhelming of such public services as roads, sewerage, and sanitation. The "beloved green spot" was transformed. In 1820 the diarist Benjamin Haydon noted that the city had "the look of manufacture and abomination."

Throughout the nineteenth and early twentieth centuries, Glasgow grew. It became one of the leading heavy engineering centers of the British Empire. Locomotives built in the city were driven in Canada, Australia, and India. Ships built on the Clyde sailed the seven seas. In 1801 the population of the city was 77,385; by 1901 this had risen to 761,709, a tenfold increase over the century. By 1931 the figure had risen to 1,088,417. Glasgow was the second biggest city in the country and one of the most important industrial cities of the British Empire.

A downturn in the city's economic fortunes occurred in the

postwar era. The whole manufacturing and shipbuilding basis of the city was undercut by shrinking markets and sharper foreign competition. Just as Glasgow was one of the leading centers of industrialization, so it became one of the more dramatic sites of deindustrialization. The city was also losing some of its vitality in the massive housing program that gave people better housing but on the giant public housing estates on the periphery or in such new towns as Cumbernauld and East Kilbride. By 1989 the population of the city had fallen to 774,008.

Things looked bleak. The city found it difficult to attract employment or capital investment. It had a reputation for hard drinking, violence, and poor housing. Throughout the 1960s and 1970s, Glasgow was regularly portrayed as a city of declining industry and rising violence. An economic and social basket case. Film crews would come up from London to point the camera at some remaining slums and get some young thugs to speak into a microphone about their violent acts. Exit film crew with the old Glasgow image unexamined and reinforced. There were even people in Glasgow who subscribed to this image. Local writers and filmmakers also helped to reproduce these images; it was their local creative seam to be mined and refined.

The dominant images began to change in the 1980s. In 1983 the city was bombarded with the elided message "Glasgow's Miles Better" (say it quickly to get the double message). This message was for internal consumption, to get the citizens to believe in the city. Later, a wider marketing campaign was launched to change the external perception of the city. Then in 1987 the city was designated the European City of Culture for 1990. This announcement did more than anything to shift public opinion. Glasgow was now sharing the same stage as Athens, Amsterdam, Florence, and Paris. During 1990 there were thirteen thousand cultural events attended by 9 million people. People began to talk of opera almost as much as soccer, and more people attended Pavarotti than the Glasgow Rangers.

The total effect was staggering in the swing of perception. Gone was the old image of Glasgow with the gangs, the violence, the hard men, and the heavy drinking. Glasgow was now seen as a pleasant, cultured city. The new man displaced the hard man.

The message of Glasgow is that images are important. In the early nineteenth century, cities needed cheap fuel and labor, easy access to raw materials, and good transport links to achieve economic growth. In the late twentieth century, they need a successful advertising campaign.

The advertising campaign was an exercise in rhetoric, a successful attempt to shift the meaning, perception, and symbolism of the city from a drab, industrial image to the sexier, culture-rich image of a postindustrial city. It was more than just rhetoric. Buildings were cleaned up, tourism was boosted, there was a renewed confidence in the city. However, and there is always a however, a cultural campaign does not fill in all the gaps left by economic disinvestment. The economic base of Glasgow is still shaky, unemployment is high, and life chances for many inhabitants are limited and constricting. The image campaign often brought these limitations into sharper relief as the people in the peripheral public housing schemes could see money spent by and for the cultural intelligentsia.

There are two responses. The first is to see the recent Glasgow experience as a successful campaign, an advertising rhetoric that worked, a turnaround in image. The second is to see it all as a cynical, superficial exercise that did not shift the economic realities or the political facts of life for a city that, despite the cleaned-up buildings, is still a black hole of contemporary capitalism. Even if successful, the selling of places is not the same as living in places. There is often a gap between the rhetoric of the advertising campaign and the texture of everyday life.

Global Village

Our view of the world is related to the means of communication. When we are limited by word of mouth, our horizons are restricted to the very local; and distant events remain just that, distant. With the development of print, messages can travel further, quicker, and more reliably. Newspapers can create a community of readers, separated by space but linked by a shared discourse. With the development of electronic media, the world is brought into our living rooms. At the flick of the button, we can see events on the other side of the world as they happen. We turn on the television and see wars and riots, elections and uprisings, protests and celebrations from around the world. Indeed, some events happen *because they are seen on television screens*. A Canadian professor, Marshall McLuhan (1964), referred to this new state of affairs as the *global village*. It was more than just technological developments in mass media. McLuhan was writing during the cold war, when the threat of mutual destruction brought to the hearts of at least one generation the extent and costs of global interdependency.

With the mass media, there is now more immediacy to our experience of distant events and a sharing of these events. The media have helped to create a new force in world affairs; global public opinion can be mobilized to release political prisoners, undermine governments, legitimize opposition movements, save the rain forest, send aid to starving peoples. For the first time in world history, the collective opinion of ordinary people has a powerful role to play in global events. Although deep divisions exist in our ability to influence events, we are all global villagers.

Our view of the world has also been affected by the new perspectives afforded by space travel. Space technology gave us the first photographs of the earth. The pictures showed a small, beautiful globe suspended in an inky darkness. National boundaries were invisible, all you could see was one world, a small vulnerable planet. A year after the first earth photograph was released, the first Earth Day was celebrated.

We now know that forest burning in one part of the world affects the climate everywhere; pollute the seas off one coastline and the whole system is affected. The world has become a collective public space, and an environmental concern has crystallized into a global awareness. There is a growing recognition of the interdependency of life on this planet.

In 1873 Jules Verne wrote a book entitled *Around the World in Eighty Days*. A modern Jules Verne would have to title his (or her) **book** *Around the World in Eighty Hours*. Places are much closer than ever before. Closer in that it takes less time to travel around the globe and closer in that there is more of a shared cultural experience. Two trends are apparent. The first is the globalization of culture. The same TV programs are seen around the world, there is a global consumption of popular music, Hollywood stars figure in the dreams of people all over the world, world novelists' works are read in the original as well as in numerous translations. There is a universal franchising of culture. The second trend is a recognition of the vernacular, a concern with the local, an emphasis on the regional. Media technology is important. National communities, no longer limited to national boundaries, are linked by videos, faxes, and telephones. A diaspora created and maintained by modern technology. The media help to sustain as well as destroy traditional communities. Some aborigines of the Australian desert are recording and communicating their dance rituals by video recorders. The traditional and the modern in an embrace of shared conflict and mutual antagonism.

Postmodernism is a response, a resistance, and a dialogue with the globalization of culture.

God

A joke from the 1960s: An astronaut comes back from a space mission. I have seen God he tells a press conference. She's black.

The image of God says as much about the existing social order as it does about the mystical order. In the last two thousand years, monotheism replaced polytheism and animism as dominant modes of religious expression. Religion was bound up with forms of social organization. The rule of patriarchy had its religious counterpart. A dominant image of God for hundreds of years portrayed an old guy with a long beard and white robe. For Christians, Jews, and Muslims alike, God was always described in the masculine. One single, essentially male God was the religious metanarrative. Other belief systems were peripheralized and marginalized. In recent years, there has been a process of religious upheaval whose nearest historical counterpart is seventeenth-century England when religious dissension flourished and debates flared up about the meaning of religious observation and practice. Today's debates are more wide ranging. The feminist critique, for example, asks why should God be a man. There has been a reassessment of the religions that existed before the male God. There is renewed interest in worship of the Goddess, Wicca, and a reevaluation of traditional belief systems. Much of the environmental movement appeals to a contemporary animism; and there has been a reaction to this splintering and fragmentation in the rise of fundamentalist beliefs. Evangelical Christianity, Orthodox Judaism, and fundamental Islam, for example, respond to the uncertainty and ambiguity of the postmodern world by claiming sanctuary in the security of fundamental belief, where doubt and uncertainty are banished. There are still many who cling to the notion of God the Father, a sort of friendly bank manager or impatient patriarch or all-knowing, all-forgiving, regular, good guy.

But the notion of God, like much else in the postmodern world, is subject to multiple interpretations, competing conceptions, alternative narratives.

Maybe the astronaut story wasn't a joke.

Holocaust

The Holocaust is the name given to the mass murders committed by the Nazis during the Second World War. It has been estimated that almost 6 million Jews were murdered. Jews were not the only ones killed. Socialists, gypsies, Communists, and homosexuals were identified, transported, and killed to "purify" a society. Etched irrevocably into the memory of the Jews, the Holocaust means many things, signifies many things; it still resonates down the years. Who cannot be moved by those flickering pictures of match-thin people in striped uniforms, with their sunken eyes reflecting unspeakable horrors?

The interpretations and reinterpretations will continue: European anti-Semitism taken to its logical, final conclusion; German barbarism; the crushing of the Other. There is also a revisionist claim that the Holocaust did not occur.

In the debate on postmodernity, the Holocaust is seen as the end point of the power of reason and the application of science bereft of humane social values. The ultimate in Othering, the end point to a system of belief that stigmatizes and ultimately denies human rights to the Other.

Science, reason, and Othering. The ingredients of modernism, baked over two hundred years, gave us liberalism, knowledge, and control over nature. They also gave us Dachau and Auschwitz.

Image

In the modern view, an image was the representation of something deeper, the surface expression of something more substantive. Image and reality were compared, contrasted, connected, and disconnected in the belief that something lay below the surface. In the postmodern world, image is all, it represents itself, it is one meaning thick. Images no longer embody information, beliefs, and values, they *are* the information, beliefs and values. The separation between the image and the message no longer exists.

Meaning has been prized from its context. We live in a world of the floating signifier. Fashion consciousness has replaced class consciousness.

There have always been people concerned with the image they portray to the rest of the world. But with the decline of simple social categories, the room for individual expression has widened. This creates uncertainty, an uncertainty that goes with choice and an uncertainty that stems from the lack of inherited images. There is now a touch of desperation in the attempt to get the right image, the most appropriate image. Politics, for example, has become less the concern with policy and more the need to construct and reconstruct political imagery. From each according to their needs, to each according to their image. The representation of images is now a dominant cultural force. Not so much the medium is the message as the image is the reality.

Industrial

In the nineteenth century, industry was associated with social change, the march of progress, a harbinger of the new social order. By the mid-twentieth century, a distinction was beginning to be drawn between old and new industry. The old was the dark, satanic mills, the forges, the clanking sounds of metal bashing, whereas the new was the odorless quiet pulse of electricity in modern factories set in landscaped parks. By the end of the twentieth century, industry is associated with the old and the past. Exceptions are made for high-tech industries, a description not so much technically accurate as socially useful to distance the new industries from the negative connotations of the old. As the economy of the rich capitalist world changed, as services became more important than manufacturing, so industry has become associated with the past, the emerging Third World, hick towns desperate for jobs. Industry is no longer a metaphor for progress, it is a symbol of stagnation. To call a city or a region "industrial" is to associate it with a set of negative images. Cities with more positive imagery are associated with the postindustrial. Industrial cities and regions are associated with the past and the old, work, pollution and the world of production, declining economic base, a city on the downward slide. The postindustrial city and region, in contrast, is associated with the new, the future, the clean, the high-tech, the economically upbeat and the socially progressive, the unpolluted, consumption and exchange, the world of leisure as opposed to work.

Intellectual

The term *intellectual* first appeared in English in 1652, used by Benlowes. Byron used it in 1813, but it came to wider usage in the nineteenth century. In Russia it was used from the 1860s onward to refer to critically thinking individuals. Through most of the modern era, intellectuals were seen as either defenders or critics of the existing social arrangements. Intellectuals tended to be university-educated, literate people who were concerned with ideas, learning, and cultural values. One populist version saw them as cultural snobs, another as persistent critics; and for many politicians, *intellectual* continues to be used as a term of abuse and criticism.

One of the more sophisticated analyses of the role of intellectuals comes from the Italian Marxist Antonio Gramsci. He was arrested by the Fascist government in 1926 and spent the rest of his life in jail. The twenty-nine notebooks he wrote while in prison constitute some of the best Marxist writing of the twentieth century. According to Gramsci, society is maintained as much by consent as by force. And this consent is a function of the power of the dominant groups to achieve hegemony in the realm of ideas and beliefs. Intellectuals have a key role in maintaining or resisting cultural hegemony. Indeed, intellectuals can be defined in relation to the production, reproduction, and consumption of hegemonic ideas and cultural values. In rural Italy of the late nineteenth and early twentieth centuries, Gramsci saw that the most powerful intellectuals were the village priests.

The modern world had a very definite view of intellectuals. They were writers, teachers, and commentators who expressed resistance or belief in modernity. They gave shape and substance to the dialogue of modernity. In the postmodern world, the meta-narratives of modernity are no longer so apparent or so compelling. The demise of socialism, the ambiguities of modernization, the acceptance and resistance to cultural globalization have all created a more fragmented worldview. There is much greater emphasis on the ephemeral, the throwaway, and the twenty-second sound bite. And the production of ideas is no longer restricted to books and journals for a minority audience. The organic intellectuals of the postmodern world are thus the scriptwriters of "soaps," journalists, talk-show hosts, compères of television quiz programs, articulate sports personalities, anchorpeople of news programs, editors and writers of such popular magazines as *Peo-*

ple and *Hello*, publicists, screenwriters and directors of popular movies, pulp fiction writers, broadcasters, pop musicians, rock stars, and famous actors and actresses. Postmodern intellectuals now have more publicists than honorary degrees and more contracts with network television than contacts with universities.

Japan

All countries are paradoxes. Some are more paradoxical than others. Japan is one such country. It is one of the most successful and richest countries. The paradox is that it is a modern country doing very well in a postmodern world. Its modernity is apparent in three things: its recent origins, its industry, and its culture.

Japan is an old country, but its institutional arrangements were forged only in the aftermath of the Second World War. Limitations were placed on the size of its armed forces and the size of its defense spending. The United States sought to limit militarism in Japanese society. What it created, and Japan was the biggest single recipient of US aid until the early 1960s, was a modern state concerned with industrial growth and economic development without the trappings of liberalism or the vestiges of feudalism. Japan was one of the truly modern states created by defeat in the Second World War.

Japan has no natural resources beyond the industry and intelligence of its people. There are no great reserves of coal, giant reservoirs of oil, or wide, wheat-growing plains. Japan used its only resources to advantage. It imported raw materials, manufactured goods, then sold them as exports. Economists call this value-added work. Japanese industry created a lot of value. In the 1950s and early 1960s, Japanese goods had a reputation for being cheap, tacky, and unreliable. They stuck with it, however, improving their products and developing quality circles in their factories, and a degree of company loyalty unmatched in the West. Japan beat its competitors at being an industrial nation. It had advantages; limited military spending meant it could spend more on the more dynamic consumer durable market. The United States built sophisticated missiles, and Japan concentrated on building cheap and reliable cars that people wanted to buy.

In a multicultural world, Japan is one of the most monocultural societies. It is one of the most homogeneous countries. The original inhabitants of the islands, the Ainu, are restricted to small numbers on Hokkaido, and "racial" purity has been maintained by severe limitations on immigration and the granting of citizenship. As the Japanese have got richer and traveled more, they have seen and been attracted to other cultures. To see hundreds of Japanese tourists at the Sagrada Familia in Barcelona or making the trek to Stratford in London or Disneyland in Los Angeles is to see the touristic results of economic power and the growing desire for overseas travel by an increasing number of Japanese. Beneath this cosmopolitanism lie both an attraction and a revulsion to multiculturalism and a taken-for-granted assumption that the Japanese are different and that to be Japanese implies a special significance.

Japan has become a model. Business leaders are keen to introduce Japanese work practices into their own countries, if not the limited salary differentials in Japanese companies; and many people look to the efficiency of Japanese industry and the sheer hard work of the population as a successful model of how to do things. But there can only be one Japan, it has become the example of successful modernity to be contrasted to the failure of modernity elsewhere and the slide into postmodernity. Rather than wish other countries to become like Japan, the interesting thing to note is how Japan is becoming like other countries. Foreign travel shows Japanese people how well other people live. They have more space, better housing, and a better quality of life than the average, hard-pressed Tokyo commuter. The hard work that was the basis for Japan's success is not built into the genes of the Japanese as many commentators assume. There is a rising gener-ation of people in Japan who take their affluence for granted, who wonder why they need to work so hard, and who think that other people should do the work. The work ethic is not so strong among young Japanese as it is for their parents. The huge trade surplus that Japanese industry created resulted in the accumu-lated funds of giant banks and the possibility of fortunes being made from financial wheeling and dealing rather than from the making and selling of things.

Jeans

"Man was born free but is everywhere in chains." This is the opening line of *The Social Contract*, written by Jean Jacques Rousseau in 1792. If he were writing today, he would amend the line to read, "People are born free but are everywhere in jeans."

Jeans are one of those bottom-up fashions that came from the ordinary folk to become one of the most universal items of cloth-ing. They are worn by rich and poor, black and white, men and women, the fashion conscious and the fashion illiterate. They can be found in the city and the country, the rich suburbs and the in-ner city, the First World and the Third World. They are worn with cheap shirts and expensive tuxedos, silk blouses, and revealing halter tops. Around the world and in all strata of society, jeans are worn. They have become the most global mode of dress.

Like much of contemporary popular culture, they originated in the United States. They were made from strong cotton fabric called denim or jean. Levi Strauss made the first pair of jeans for miners in the California gold rush of the 1850s. Since then their use has spread around the world and percolated through most social hierarchies. Is there anyone in the Western world who has never worn a pair of jeans? Of course there are jeans and there are jeans. Jeans have been straight and bell-bottomed, baggy and tight, and have even been given the name of fashionable designers. These latter look like ordinary jeans but are twice the price, perhaps to pay for all those erotic advertising campaigns. The wearing of jeans links people around the world. I remember seeing the fall of the Berlin Wall. All those East Germans wearing jeans made them seem just like you or me. But we knew how backward and repressed they were because the only jeans they were wearing were those dated, stone-washed, streaky type.

Given the ambiguities at the heart of postmodernity, it should not strike us as strange that the local and the global go hand in hand. Just as people are resurrecting local cultures, regional cuisines, and old dialects, they are also all wearing jeans. "Dress global and act local" could be one of the catch phrases of postmodernity. Jeans have become the most global mode of dress capable of infinite variety and endless variation. A mark of resistance and individuality they are also a symbol of global conformity and mass consumption. To wear jeans is to be both an individual and yet part of global consumption and mass display. As Karl Marx should have said, "People of the world unite, you have nothing to lose but your jeans."

Kurds

There are almost 25 million Kurds. By all accounts the Kurds should have passed into obscurity. Originally nomadic herdspeople, they inhabited the mountain region in Southwest Asia that used to be called Kurdistan. The Kurds lost out in the division of the area into separate states after the First World War. Kurdistan was eventually divided up by the Soviet Union, Turkey, Iran,

Syria, and Iraq. The Kurds were scattered throughout these different states. They were an anomaly in the modern world, preindustrial in an industrial age, Sunni Muslims at a time of secularization and a nation without a state. Their continued existence is an embodiment and reflection of the postmodern world, where religion is resurging and nationalism is flourishing. But a nation without a state still has tremendous difficulties. None of the states are willing to give up territory for the Kurds, who have few sources of power or influence. They are used by the great powers for their own ends. The United States helped Saddam Hussein discipline the Kurds when the United States wanted an ally against Iran; the United States then encouraged Kurdish nationalism in 1991 during the Desert Storm campaign, only to abandon them after the brief war was over. The postmodern world may be different from the modern world, but not that different. The weak and the powerless still get shafted.

As *National Geographic* reported in 1992:

> The Kurds are homeless even at home, and stateless abroad. Their ancient woes are locked inside an obscure language. They have powerful, impatient enemies and a few rather easily bored friends. Their traditional society is considered as a nuisance at worst and a curiosity at best. For them the act of survival, even identity itself, is a kind of victory.

Lifestyle

It sounds like the name of one of those glossy magazines with a brash, publicity-seeking editor, lots of pictures of women with small waists and big breasts and men with granite-like jaws and rock-solid pectorals all wrapped up in an editorial policy that decries sexism. It probably is the name of one of those glossy magazines with a brash, publicity-seeking editor, lots of . . .

Lifestyle has become one of the most-used postmodern words because there is no longer either the security or the restriction of narrowly defined social roles that cover a wide variety of practices. When there was only rich, poor, and an aspiring middle, things were easier. Depending on which class you were in, you lived in certain areas, ate certain types of food, dressed in specific ways, even talked in social dialects and took your vacations at particular times in particular resorts. The solid divisions of the past have been undermined by the instability of the present. You can still tell the very rich and the very poor, but away from these extremes it is more and more difficult. There has been a democratization of style, a toning down of conspicuous consumption; the rich dress down while the poor dress up. In the realm of consumption, and we are what we consume, there is a much more complex semiotics of class and social position. The lifestyle-type magazines seek to describe the new syntax of style. With the rigid rules of tradition no longer in operation, people have more choices. The richer you are the more choices you have. You are a man in your twenties and work in business. You could have the preppy look, the serious business look, the radical mover-and-shaker look with its touches of outre fashion, the working-class hero look. So many looks. The awful anxiety of freedom and choice. Lifestyle is the name given to the choices, the various options, and the temporary decisions.

Marxism

This was one of the great religions of the modern period. It was the opium of the intellectuals, a science of society and history that claimed to understand the profane present and inaugurate the sacred future. The prophet was Karl Marx (1818–83), one of the most underrated thinkers of the nineteenth century but one of the most overrated thinkers of the twentieth century. With a combination of German philosophy, French socialism, and English economics, Marx provided one of the best and most sustained analyses of contemporary capitalism. His writings have a depth, a flair, and an attention to scholarly detail that are rarely matched. He saw the emerging working class as a vital social force able to transform society toward the promised land of communism. His ideas were diffused around the world and gave the intellectual backbone to a whole series of resistances and rebellions against the new capitalist order. His ideas were used, abused, codified, and transformed into Marxism, capable of multiple interpretations that sustained some of the best and justified some of the worst social movements of the twentieth century. Marxism was at its best when it was the voice of resistance, the critical solvent of the existing order. When it became the ruling force, the dominant ideology, it was used to justify totalitarian regimes around the world. The People's Democratic Republics were neither democratic nor republican and had more to do with a ruling elite than the people. For most of those in the East, Marxism was the doctrine of repression. For some in the West, it was the call to revolution, an insistence that there was a better alternative. The flawed experience and the fall of communism have turned the shining metal of Marxism into a rusty old hunk of scrap that is being junked around the world. There are still a few Marxists; fighters in the Andes, revolutionaries in the desiccated plains of East Africa, and some tenured faculty in prestigious universities in the West. But for most, Marxism was the God that failed. Another great universal narrative has been abandoned.

Modernism

We can make a distinction between modernism and modernity. Modernism is an aesthetic sensibility whose roots include such revolutionary movements as impressionism, futurism, and surrealism in the visual arts, atonalism in music, functionalism in architecture, experimentalism and the antinaturalism in the modern novel. It has a time and a place; the turn of the nineteenth into the first half of the twentieth century. Essentially European in its early origins, it found a comfortable home in the United States. It involved a break with the past and the emergence of an artistic elite separated out from the rest of society. It involved the creation of Art from art and Artists from artisans. The modern artist became the new hero of bourgeois sensitivities, giving a personal shape to the collective anguish of the modern world. Modernism disturbed the present by denying the past.

Modernity

Modernity is the historical context of modernism, a time of rapid industrialization, large-scale urbanization, the destruction of traditional societies, the creation of a global economy. It has roots far back in history.

All dates are arbitrary. Fourteen ninety-two is as good as any. In 1492 the "New World" was captured, controlled, named, and incorporated into a world economy, whose center was Europe and whose periphery was being created around the world. In the ensuing centuries, the periphery was enlarged. First Central America, then South America, India, Australia, Africa, Asia. Despite resistance and in some cases rebellion, European dominance was extended and strengthened around the world. Traditional societies have been altered, a global economy created, and a worldview constructed. It is the view of the winners, those at the top of the international division of labor. History has become the story of the diffusion of civilization out from the epicenter of Europe. The story creates the Other—the blacks, the natives, the backward looking, and the savages—different names but the same designation. Light and dark given human representation across the world; ego and id condensed in the historical geography of the modern world.

Modernity embodied a view of history. Premodern was the past relegated to the glass case of anthropological concern, interesting only as a measure of the level of progress, a mark of how far we had come. The future was the upward continuation of the modern present into the better future.

Multiculturalism

In a postimperial, postcolonial world, European civilization is no longer assured a position of superiority. There is now a more general acceptance of the existence, integrity, and worth of other cultures. The safeguarding and celebration of cultural diversity is the essence of multiculturalism. Multiculturalism discourages racist beliefs and racist practices; as the name implies, its basic tenet is that there is more than one culture. While some may have more influence than others, they are all of equal value. In this new mind-set, cultural diversity is now seen as a worthwhile goal and cultural heterogeneity rather than cultural homogeneity is seen as the desired state.

The persistence of racist beliefs and practices undermines the goal of multiculturalism. While many people may want to attend a variety of "ethnic" festivals, the same people may still like to live in suburbs of like-minded, like-looking people. In many instances multiculturalism is no more than rhetoric. I avoid the use of the term *mere rhetoric*, however, because all social changes begin with new words, new stories, and new ways of describing the world. Rhetoric is always the first stage in social change.

Multiculturalism is also part of the redefinition of culture. It collapses the notion of a hierarchy of culture with European ways at the apex. Take music. No longer is European music seen as the standard. The development of "world music" is an acceptance of the diversity of human musical creativity. A postmodern musical outfit could embrace mouth music, Amazonian drumming, symphonic percussion, didgeridoo, guitars, and a computer-assisted music machine. Multiculturalism is also part of that questioning of the demarcation between high and low culture, highbrow and popular, with the associated value judgments that this division implies. If Inuit mouth music, Amazonian drumming or didgeridoo playing is seen as legitimate music, it then becomes more and more difficult to maintain the fiction that symphony music is superior to country and western just because it is a symphony.

The practice of multiculturalism is an enterprise fraught with difficulty. Take hiring practices. To achieve a better racial balance, should governments and institutions promote the use of quotas? This has problems. Positive discrimination implies a discrimination against someone else. This is a fact that some proponents of multiculturalism have difficulty in accepting. They thus find it difficult to understand the white backlash to positive discrimination for blacks in the United States. Moreover, such schemes do not help "blacks." They help certain people who are black. For example, positive discrimination in universities for the admission of black students does not help the whole black population. It helps the children of the black middle class. Considering these problems does not invalidate the goal or practice of multiculturalism. It just means we need a more realistic view of the problems, paradoxes, and ambiguities of all attempts to turn noble causes into workable programs.

At its very best, multiculturalism is the celebration of the diversity of the human family and an affirmation of the unity of the human condition.

Museums

The form of new buildings or the change of use of old buildings tells us much. One of the great railway stations of Paris was the Gare d'Orsay, a grand architectural statement of the nineteenth century, full of optimism about the future, a celebration of progress and modernity. In the 1970s it was scheduled for demolition. No longer useful as a railway terminal, it was considered functionally obsolete. By 1977, however, the tide of official opinion had shifted. Obsolete as a train station, it was culturally important enough to be "saved" and designated a museum of art. The glass of the curved ceilings looks down no longer on steam engines and hurrying passengers but on beautiful impressionist canvases and the swirling crowds of art lovers. The transformation of the Gare d'Orsay into the Musée d'Orsay is part of the postmodern turn, part of the constant looking forward and the belief in progress, part of a more ambiguous concern with the past as well as the future, with maintaining rather than demolishing fragments of the past and with the historicizing of place and time: railway stations into museums, coal mines into theme parks, industrial warehouses into arts centers, and theme parks into places of historic importance. The recycling of the past, the new use of old buildings, and the backward glance that drive the museumification of our lives are part of the paradox of postmodernity, that steady forward movement into the re-created, reconstructed past.

Nationalism

Throughout most of the twentieth century, it was assumed by many that nationalism was an old-fashioned concept with little place in the modern world. Both of the dominant ideologies, capitalist free markets and state socialism, looked forward in their different ways to a world where national boundaries had little place. The capitalists hoped for a global market, free of tariff barriers; and the socialists looked forward to a society of universal citizenship. In the modernist conception, nationalism was an atavistic remnant of an older world. But nationalism has proved more resilient than the modern critics first thought. Especially in Europe, the continent of its birth. In Eastern Europe it is reemerging from the confines of state socialism. And in Western Europe, the strengthening of the European Community has allowed nationalist sentiments buried by the great nation-states of Britain, France, Spain, and Italy to reappear.

The renewal of the nationalist enterprise is part of a broader move from a concern with space, with universals and with the forward march of history to a concern with place, with more local identities and folk memories. Modernism looked forward to a more uniform world. The postmodern world is one where individual identity is based more on a hierarchy of levels, global and national and local. There is much to celebrate in this shift. There is also much to fear. Nationalism is a form of group identity that excludes others. Nationalism defines an "in group" and an "out group," definitions not innocent of implications. Just ask the people in what used to be Yugoslavia.

New Age

New Age covers a variety of things from tarot readings, channeling, numerology, astrology, and holistic medicine to a belief in reincarnation, karmic influences, and cosmic harmonics. Gurus include Shirley Maclaine and Linda Goodman. New Age is a mixture of old, half-forgotten folk knowledge and prescientific beliefs and practices brought up to date for the contemporary seekers of wisdom, self-knowledge, and understanding. New Age shows the powerful hidden forces in the world affecting the individual and also a belief in the ability of the individual to affect these influences. The growing importance of New Age beliefs is a reflection of the failure of orthodox religion and science to provide meaning and understanding. The modern solution was to have a belief in the power of progress, of the ability of the future to transcend the problems of the present. New Age signifies a return to the past, a resurrection and reconstruction of alternative belief systems and old understandings, a creative excavation of the layers of knowledge that existed before the dominance of scientific rationality. For its adherents the New Age is a widening of our vision, an extension of our knowledge beyond the narrowing confines of a mechanistic Cartesian universe into a wider, deeper, fuller understanding of the rich complexity of the world. For its critics, the New Age is just a bunch of weirdos, irrational and unenlightened, looking for the solution to their problems in the action of the stars, the precise numbers of their car registration, or the colors of the clothes they wear.

New Man

The new man is man in the world after feminist critique. A world where masculinity is no longer the virile force it used to be. Traditional concepts of manliness have been undermined, criticized, and reviled. Patriarchy, the rule of men, is blamed by some for everything from the arms race to the hole in the ozone layer. Men feel under attack. Not just from women. There is an emerging men's movement that seeks to outline new role models, replacing the unfettered Hero with the tolerant King, the wise Magician and the sensitive Lover. Writers like Robert Bly and Sam Keen are trying to plot a new path for the new man. As befits the postmodern turn, it is a path full of paradox and ambiguity, a spiral rather than a straight line. Sam Keen writes of a move from having the answers to living the questions, from emotional numbness to manly grief, from false optimism to honest despair and from artificial toughness to virile fear. Aaron Kipnis writes of an integrated masculinity that is neither hard nor soft but flexible; neither bastard nor nice guy but fierce, neither patriarchal nor matriarchal but polytheistic.

There are in fact three new men. The first, desperate to deflect criticism of being a chauvinist, hides his masculinity in a politically correct attitude. He is basically frightened of women. The second new man is antifeminist. But unlike the old man, he knows that what he is saying and doing is subject to attack and criticism. This new man parades his aggressive masculinity with a shaky self-confidence. He is also basically frightened of women but goes on the offensive. The third new man half-fears, half-loves women. He knows about the injustices but does not feel it is all his fault. He wants to accommodate the feminist position without becoming bogeyman, victim, or oppressor. He feels his masculinity is under some kind of vague threat but thinks that women both desire and reject his male power. Some men can be all three or some combination depending on the time, place, and company.

The world is very confusing for the new man. He is trying to be both man and human, to accept both the limits and the opportunities of his manliness, to extend the experience of his life beyond the narrow confines of restricted stereotypical roles; but as yet he has few role models, little experience, and no road map.

Nouvelle Cuisine

A narrow definition: nouvelle cuisine emerged in the 1960s in France as a reaction to a style of cooking in which things were presented with rich, heavy, masking sauces. Cooks like Paul Bocuse, Fernand Point, Jean and Pierre Troisgros used fresh ingredients to create food that was lighter, less hidden by sauces, and beautifully presented. The aesthetics of the food was just as important as the nutritional count. Dishes became works of art, sparse, light, and in the best restaurants very, very expensive.

A broader definition: nouvelle cuisine is one strand, albeit one of the earliest and best known of the shifts in eating patterns and food consumption that are part of the postmodern turn. Postmodern cuisine is concerned with fresh, local ingredients. The freshness cites the natural; and the reversal of CULTURE-nature to NATURE-culture is at the heart of the postmodern critique. The local ingredients cite place rather than space, the unique in contrast to the general. This is but one of the responses to the globalization of food consumption. On the one hand, McDonalds are sprouting up everywhere, while on the other, there is a return to the uniqueness of regional and national dishes.

Another important element in the new cuisine of postmodernity is the mixing of dishes, Thai salsa, Tex-Mex, and so on. The combination of regional and national styles is a culinary multiculturalism, an eclecticism of the palate that mirrors and embodies the ragout of postmodernity.

Cooking and eating are important defining elements in the social and cultural identification. You are what you eat, when you eat, and how you eat. The consumption of food is an important element in the definition of class position, a reassertion of ethnic identity, and a source of community bonding and social difference. Nouvelle cuisine has become the internationally accepted form of upmarket food consumption. Around the expensive restaurants of the world, the affluent are eating low-calorie, beautifully presented, high-cost food. This consumption intersects with other discourses—the body beautiful, light as opposed to heavy, food as art rather than food as fuel.

Office

The office has replaced the factory as the dominant site of work and social interaction outside the home. In the nineteenth and early twentieth centuries, industry was a major economic enterprise. Men working in factories was one of the defining elements of modernity. In recent years, however, there has been a deindustrialization in the rich capitalist countries. Factories have closed and the traditional male working class has been reduced to social insignificance and political impotence. People working in offices now dominate the working scene. The "office" is the working environment of an increasing number of people.

In the typical corporation, position in the hierarchy is registered by the size and location of your office. Routine office workers share large rooms with little privacy. The chief executives get the biggest offices at the top of the building. Here, entry has to be negotiated through an outer office guarded by a secretary. You just can't walk in. You have to make an appointment and wait until they can see you. Your time has to match their convenience. Zones of space and time have to be traversed before the inner sanctum is reached. Here, far from the ground and close to the sky, noise is kept to a minimum by the dampening effect of thick, expensive carpets; and the walls are covered with expensive "art." People move slowly, talk in hushed tones. This is top executive space. But if you listen, you can hear the gentle hum of flattery, deception, intrigue, and diplomacy as people seek to align themselves with the trajectories of power and influence.

Office politics are different from the old factories because men and women work together in the office. Traditional patterns of male dominance are often reinforced—the male boss and female secretary pattern—but only occasionally undercut. The office is the main site for gender relations outside the home. Sexual politics, sexual harassment, and gender relations are embodied and resisted in the office.

Technology has allowed the dispersal of people and activities. Telephones, faxes, computer linkups, conference calls, modems, and networks now allow many people to stay at home; to create an "office" in the "home" and thus privatize the collective experience of work. This gives more freedom but less physical contact. The office has become an idea, an arena, a point of connection, both physical and technical, with the outside world.

Ozone

Ozone is a form of oxygen. If this were a technical A to Z, I would mention that it has three atoms in the molecule, is an unstable gas with a distinctively fresh smell, formed in the atmosphere by the action of solar light on oxygen. But ozone is as much a cultural phenomenon as a chemical one. It has become a symbol of the global environmental crisis. Ozone shields us from the harmful effects of ultraviolet radiation. We "knew" this scientifically, but it did not become a major issue until the subject of the depletion of ozone became an item of interest to the international news media and then a focus of world concern. Pollutants from the earth are, it is argued by many, causing a thinning of the protective ozone shield. There is some evidence to suggest that the negative effects are beginning to show up in greater incidences of skin cancer. Decades of sun worship may slowly be coming to an end. An end to the bronzed beautiful.

Ozone has become a metaphor for environmental deterioration. Even as something as seemingly benign as the domestic refrigerator is a cause of ozone depletion. It seems that we can only keep our lettuce crisp by frying the surface of the earth. Our present economic systems are destructive of the earth. Whether we can change before it is too late is the new metanarrative, the global imperative, and the most universal of concerns.

Patriarchy

Patriarchy is the systematic domination of women by men. One historical view looks back to the Golden Age from about 25,000 years ago to 500 B.C. when many communities saw God as a woman and Goddess worship was common. Womanhood was given a sacred status. With the rise of Islam, Judaism, and Christianity, a female deity was replaced by a male God. God the Father rather than God the Mother. Since then history (rather than herstory) has been, according to feminists, a domination of women by men in the sphere of religious symbolism, systems of knowledge, sexuality, fertility, and political practices of exclusion and marginalization. Patriarchy is thus a system of power, a mode of representation, and a legitimizing of inequality; it is both a practice of domination and a belief in the biological basis of gender inequality.

For many, patriarchy is a bad thing. In one extreme position, patriarchy is the source of all ills, including pollution, war, consumerism, disease, and suffering. This is an attractive position because it exonerates approximately half the population from any wrongdoing. The other half are thus to blame for everything. The extreme counterposition is to dismiss any systematic bias against women. I am uncomfortable with either extreme.

Patriarchy is a system of power that distorts and stunts the full development of both men and women. Neither can achieve full potential as human beings in a patriarchal system. Patriarchy is not so much the rule of men as the rule of little boys.

Political Correctness

This is one of the attitudes most closely associated with the debate on multiculturalism. A politically incorrect joke would combine sexism, racism, and ageism in one punch line!

To demean people because of such attributes as race, age, gender, and sexual orientation is the enemy of political correctness. Like all countervailing movements, political correctness—shortened by some to PC—has its fair share of both worthies and loonies. Our language, our belief systems, indeed our whole societies have an Othering quality that degrades some people, marginalizes some, and ignores others. PC at its best makes us more sensitive to this tendency. At its worst it has a Fascist quality. We can all be tolerant with nice people. The real mark of tolerance is to be able to find a space for people you don't like, don't trust, and can't understand. Free speech is an easy principle to uphold if the speaker is saying something you want to hear. It is a more difficult principle to believe in or to support if someone is saying something you do not want to hear. Should we give a platform to racists and homophobes? To answer yes or no is easy. To understand the implications of the answer is much more difficult.

Postmodern

As an adjective *postmodern* is used to describe all manner of things, ideas, trends, and fads. It is used with reference to almost anything that is eclectic, multicultural, heterogeneous, varied, different. Let's get a better handle through comparisons. James Joyce is a modernist novelist, whereas postmodern novelists would include Milan Kundera and Julian Barnes. Shostakovitch is a modern composer, Philip Glass is a postmodern composer. Picasso is a modernist; Papunya sand paintings by aborigines from central Australia would constitute postmodern art. Mies van der Rohe is a modern architect, Arata Isozaki is a postmodern architect.

Postmodern is also more generally used to refer to the new, the contemporary, the paradoxical, the ambiguous, the weird, the strange, the mixtures and combinations of old and new, universal and vernacular, ancient and modern, good taste and bad taste, something new, and the same old thing, something radically different and historically repetitive. It derives from the historical period known as . . .

Postmodernity

This is the time after modernity. The *post* suggests that something has changed: a reaction to the formalism of modernism; a loss in the belief in progress, reason, and universal truth; a resistance to the traditional patterns of dominance of Eurocentrism, patriarchy, and "expertise"; a concern with the past as much as with the future; a consideration of the vernacular as much as of the universal; a concentration on particular places rather than on abstract spaces; a resistance to the notion of modernization; a contestation with the metanarratives of science and Marxism; a distrust in the idea of universal values; a disbelief in the concept of transcendent, immanent Truth.

Postmodernity, compared to modernity, has neither the same reading of history nor the same belief in the future. Postmodernity is the ambiguous present, the present imperfect compared to the present perfect of modernity.

Quilts

In 1971 the Whitney Museum of American Art put on an exhibition entitled "Abstract Designs in American Quilts." It consisted of sixty quilts, the earliest dated 1850 and the most recent 1920.

These quilts were made by ordinary people by stitching layers of material. They were practical, essential in a cold climate, but also decorative; the designs ranged from the highly abstract to the representational, and they came in a rich range of colors. In the past they had been seen simply as pieces of craft and, if they were shown at all, they were displayed in folk museums or craft fairs.

The Whitney is a modern piece of brutalist architecture in the heart of Manhattan with a reputation for showing some of the most uncompromising examples of modern art. Jaspar Johns, Mark Rothko, and Jackson Pollock are just some of the artists whose work hangs on bare concrete walls. For this museum to show "folk art" was a departure that marks the beginning of postmodernism. The exhibition destroyed the distinction between art and craft, erased the demeaning qualifier of "folk" from "folk art," and opened up a whole new discourse of what constituted art, culture, and the American artistic heritage. It is a delicious irony that cultural postmodernism had one of its early tryouts in one of the most modernist museums in a city with such a strong association with modernism.

A footnote. Some of the quilts in the exhibition were originally bought for as little as $10. Today, those selfsame quilts cost thousands of dollars. The art of the people can become the collections of the wealthy. *See also* Commodification.

Another footnote. The experience of AIDS and the making of quilts has come together in the construction of the AIDS quilt, a memorial to the people who have died from AIDS. The combined quilt now stretches over acres of ground that would fill fifteen football stadiums.

Race

At the end of the nineteenth century, many social commentators in the West used race as a biological category, a defining element in explaining levels of civilization; modes of behavior; level of cultural attainment; and, ultimately, to explain the relative ranking of races with regard to political and economic power. At the end of the twentieth century, race has a more problematic position. Race has become "race," the quotation marks signaling the difficulty. "Race" is now seen by many commentators as more a social construct than a biological fact. Race is socially constructed rather than biologically determined. Arguments that use biological race as a determining element in explaining levels of achievement, social progress, and educational attainment are classified as racist and dismissed as politically incorrect. "Race" as a social construct, however, is seen as an important element in the functioning of societies. The racial bias of social practices and knowledge systems is vigorously contested. And there is an important politics of naming. Many in the United States, for example, prefer to use the term *African-American* rather than *black*. One distinguishes by origin, the other assumes a biological category.

There is now a reassertion of the importance of "racial differences," the need to include other "races" in any understanding of the human condition, an openness to the expression of voices not heard before. Hence, the importance of "minority" voices, whether it be the recognition given to aboriginal art in Australia and "black" female writers around the world, or the greater sensitivity shown toward the story of the Native American Indian in the creation of the United States. As a site of resistance rather than as a biological determinant, "race" has added to the plurality of voices in the cacophony of postmodernism.

Religion

For the modernists religion was a remnant of an old order, a fragment of tradition that would be swept away by the enlightened

sumerist economic system and a cultural system that is concerned with undermining the metanarrative. When our experience can no longer be fitted under the big story, the categories continue to disintegrate. The term *people* hides the difference between men and women, but gender alone fails to distinguish by race, which does not begin to consider sexual orientation, which ignores the differences caused by place, time, and cohort. And so it goes on until the only story of meaning is my story. The only legitimate voice is my own. This is liberating. It is also painful. An intentional subjectivity makes us responsible for everything in our lives. Hence, the explosion in the number and consumption of *self*-help and *self*-improvement books. Our lives are the lived self, our world is collapsed into a narrow, insecure niche of controlling subjectivity. When we can no longer use the collective myths or social rituals, we lose a refuge as well as a prison, we miss a support as well as a restraint. Walls keep us in, but they also support our weight. The contemporary interest in aesthetic reflexivity, individual identity, and the biographical nature of the self is a danger as well as an opportunity. A liberation from the collective, the group, and the shared story can also mean a lonely individualism. The first wave of postmodernity has shown us the differences between us and what separates us out one from another; the next wave may try to reconstruct these individualized selves into communities of resistance and tolerance. When too much space is created between people, the result is not freedom but silent space. The next major social project is how to link together the exposed subjective experiences with new, liberating, collective discourses.

Semiotics

Semiotics is the science of signs. It is concerned with decoding all the multiple and varied meanings involved in the different systems of communication. When we think of the word sign, often the image of a traffic *sign* appears. *Stop. No Right Turn. No Parking.* These are signs with a definite message. You do not have to have a Ph.D. in applied semiotics to know what *No Parking* means.

Most signs are more subtle. We communicate with each other in all kinds of ways. Direct speech, texts, music, clothing, gestures, food. They all have meanings associated with them. Take food. In India some people will not eat sacred cows; in England people will not knowingly eat horse meat; yet, in France it is considered more acceptable. In neither European country is the eating of dogs considered fashionable or acceptable. The difference between cows, horses, and dogs lies not in their respective nutritional value but in what they signify in the different cultures.

Semiotics started in linguistics, and its earliest applications were in the realm of language. An influential figure was Ferdinand de Saussure (1857–1913), the Swiss linguist who said that signs were arbitrary. It is by convention that the term *dog* conjures up images of the animal we call *dog*. It could just have easily been called odg. There is no necessary relationship between the signifier, the word *dog*, and the signified, the animal with four legs that barks. Semiotics was extended beyond linguistics by such figures as Roland Barthes (1915–80). Barthes looked at striptease performances, Citroen cars, and images of Einstein's head as signs full of cultural and social meaning. Semiotics has become more central to intellectual pursuits in the postmodern world. The concept of arbitrary signifiers appeals to the more postmodern view of the world that rejects universal standards of "right" clothing, "correct" food consumption, and so forth. Semiotics thus allows the multiplicity of meanings and varied signification systems to be studied and discussed. We now live in a world of the floating signifier. Signifier and signified have been prized from their historical context. Semiotics shows that there is no one system of signification. Dogs are eaten in the Philippines, not because the people are savages, but because they do not embody the same deep meaning of pets and thus of animals physically and emotionally closer to humans as they do in England or France. Semiotics does not rank systems of signification. There may be dominant cultures but no "right" cultures. Today, there is a welter of images, competing messages, and multiple systems of signification. We live in a world of semiotic overload.

Sexuality

We live in a post-Freudian world. Sexuality is no longer the stuff of repressed dreams; long, thin objects in dreams are no longer the symbol of the penis. In many dreams today, the penis appears as a penis. In contrast to the turn-of-the-century Viennese bourgeoisie, many of us no longer need to camouflage our sexual fantasies.

The world is saturated in sexuality. Naked bodies are constantly on display in movies, television, and advertising. Sexuality has broken away from the straitjacket of Victorian prudery. Daytime talk shows regularly discuss a range of sexual fantasies and practices from women falling in love with their fathers to adult men who want to be dressed up in baby clothes. Incest and infantile fantasies as family "entertainment." Alternative sexualities are less hidden and in some cases provide a basis for individual identity and group cohesion; *gay, lesbian,* and even the stronger terms of *queer* and *dyke* have been used with open pride as qualifying adjectives for things as varied as writings and text, neighborhoods, bars, and holiday resorts. Full tolerance is not yet a reality; but compared to even fifty years ago, the more open nature of sexual discourse is a social change of revolutionary magnitude. The revolution is not everywhere as even and deep as in other places. Gay issues are more openly discussed in San Francisco and Amsterdam than they are in Cleveland or Newcastle. There is a backlash. In some places gay bashing becomes more prevalent the more "public" gays become, and moral entrepreneurs are always on hand to invest people's sexual fears and anxieties into homophobia.

Traditional definitions of socially acceptable sexuality are being contested and reappraised. Sexual discourses become more public and more visible as more people define themselves either in part or in whole by their sexuality. Coming out of the closet, whether the closet be homosexuality, "different" sexual practices, or sexual fantasies of an unusual kind, is an act of self-definition. Sexual orientation, as much as gender, race, and class, has become one of the defining elements of social heterogeneity. Combinations of these elements are providing new voices. The black female lesbian, for example, can give a perspective on race, gender, and sexual persuasion that has rarely been heard. These "new" voices are illuminating the things that keep us apart as well as bind us together.

One of the metanarratives of the modern world was a definition of legitimate sexuality. There was a definite core of socially sanctioned sexuality and an illegitimate, and in some cases illegal, periphery. The postmodern world in many other respects is less of a core-periphery and more of a series of peripheries. The notion of a solid core is being criticized. The term *straight* can be sometimes heard with a tone of rebuke.

There is a shadow. The spectre of AIDS hangs over the sexual revolution, a backlash of fundamentalist beliefs is creating a discourse of complaint and criticism, while the commodification of sexuality leads to pornography as well as exploitation. Despite all of this, sexuality has lost some of its Freudian heaviness. When Dykes on Bikes ride alongside the Sisters of Perpetual Indulgence in a march of gay pride, we know that sexual orientation has lost some of its power to shame. The fun of sexuality, as well as its politics and culture, is part of postmodernity. It is connected with other discourses, the cult of the body, the emphasis on pleasure rather than redemptive suffering, and the concern with subjective experience rather than collective rituals. Know Thyself has been replaced with Satisfy Yourself. The repression of the past has been replaced with the openness of the present, Dr. Ruth Westheimer has replaced Dr. Sigmund Freud, and the art of arousal has displaced the science of psychoanalysis.

Superficial

If you think the term *superficial* is a criticism, then you are still a modernist. For postmodernists, what you see is what there is. There is no deeper, underlying reality, no invisible structure that gives meaning and coherence to the world. Surface appearances are surface realities. Superficiality is not something to be avoided, it is something to be attained. Like this entry; glib, cute, and utterly ephemeral.

Text

If you think that the word *text* means books or manuscripts, then you are a modernist. For the postmodernist, texts can be anything from books to movies, postcards to songs, gardens to cities, advertising jingles to holidays. Postmodernism has extended the usual definition of *texts* to include . . . well, almost everything. The idea of texts as only books is seen as an elitist, Eurocentric, a monocultural definition of art, creativity, authorship, and readership. With the collapse of the distinction between "high" art and "popular" culture and the belief that narratives of power and domination are inscribed in most objects and practices, then the whole world is a text to be written as well as read. The production of texts is part of the creation and maintenance of a community. In the postmodern world, communities of resistance, which contest the dominant narratives, have flourished. The return to ethnic roots, the writing of alternative histories, the (re-)creation of different cultures are all inscribed in texts. At one and the same time, there are the global texts and the more local texts. General and specific, space and place.

The consumption of texts is not a passive acceptance but a creative act. In the postmodern world, texts are taken apart (deconstructed) by an observer. There are communities of consumption that give shape and difference to the world. Global texts, such as big Hollywood movies, are consumed differently, they mean different things to different audiences. The global consumption connects the world, the differing interpretations separate the world.

Television

Television is the transmittal and receival of radio waves. A product of the twentieth century, it has become the mass form of entertainment and communication. For many cultural critics, television led to the blandification of culture, a retreat to the lowest common denominator. I do not think so. To be sure television in the United States, driven almost entirely by commercial considerations, is overwhelmingly awful. There are few redeeming features to a cultural form so devoid of critical content and continually ruptured by crude advertising. Some excellent programs are made; but their whole timing, rhythm, and cadence are destroyed by crassly timed and frequent commercial breaks (*see also* Zapper).

In Europe and North America, television viewing patterns have changed dramatically in the last few years. Television was first introduced in the 1950s; and for the next thirty years, it was a shared ritual. Programs came on at specific times. People made appointments with the medium to be there at the time their favorite show was aired. Popular programs were watched by millions of people; they were part of a shared culture, a shared sense of identity, a National Theater, a National Debate, a National Entertainment all rolled into one. The major television programs were a source of gossip, shared experience, part of the cement that gave coherence to the structure of society. Things began to change in the 1980s. There were more channels, more choices, and the huge audiences were still huge but they were watching different programs. Videos allowed programs to be watched at the viewer's convenience, an appointment system was replaced by a demand system, public debates by private pleasures. The proliferation and fragmentation of viewing audiences was part cause and part effect of a decline of nationally homogeneous consumption patterns. Television reflected and embodied the postmodern fracturing and fragmentation as universal viewing patterns were replaced by a more varied, heterogeneous pattern of television consumption. At times of national emergencies, great political events, or occasions of high drama, mass television watching of the same programs could bring a people together in the shared communion of television consumption. But these were the exceptions not the rule. More individualized forms of consumption were replacing mass forms of consumption. People were watching different programs, at different times and in different ways. The television is no longer a social glue, the cultural hearth of the home; it has become a multi-audienced medium and just one more appliance of domestic pleasure and instruction. The product of modern technology has become a source of the postmodern rupture.

Third World

The term originated in the 1950s in France. It was used to refer to the poor countries of the world. The First World consisted of the rich capitalist countries and the Second was composed of the socialist bloc. It is now so widely used that it has become an adjective; Third World economy, Third World plumbing, Third World conditions. It is generally used to mean poor.

The term has an important connotation. It implies that the Third World is somehow separate from the rest of the world. It indicates that these conditions of poverty are unconnected to the conditions of wealth, that the Third World is some historical remnant of a poorer time. The term *underdeveloped country* gives the same impression; the poverty of an underdeveloped country is because it is backward, it has not yet caught up with the West, it is still stuck in the past. This is an international blame-the-victim scenario. They are poor because they are not like us, and they are not like us because they are poor. They inhabit a different world. A Third World. An alternative explanation posits that the historical functioning and present arrangement of the world economy operates to transfer wealth from poor to rich countries. Underdevelopment is created. Countries are not naturally poor or historically poor, they are made poor by their role and position in the world economy. World poverty is connected to world wealth, the First and Third Worlds are misnomers, the rich and poor inhabit the same world. The term *Third World* ignores and disguises the links that connect rich and poor, poverty and plenty, us and them.

Truth

There isn't any. Well not in the modern conception of one truth or truths out there waiting to be uncovered. Some philosophers, notably Richard Rorty, have disputed the notion of truth being a representation of a reality in nature. Truth is more appropriately seen as a provisional, pragmatic agreement that is subject to revision and change. Without the confidence of being Right, reality is capable of multiple truths. Indeed, there are multiple realities. Without the benefit of a universal credo, the world is subject to a more fragmented, contested number of different interpretations.

Truth, like reality, just isn't what it used to be.

United States

To fly across the Midwest of the United States on a cloudless day is to see the reflection of liberal rationalism on the surface of the earth. Mile after mile of mathematically formulated subdivisions crisscross the land. To find your way in most US cities is relatively easy. Most of them have a grid-pattern system of streets, in which north-south roads meet east-west streets to form giant square blocks.

The United States is one of the most *modern* countries. Its political philosophy like its landscape has a belief in order, in progress, in the redeeming quality of individual effort and the possibility of civic improvement. From 1776 to the present day, a continuous line can be drawn between then and now that links ideas of the minimal state, the concern with individual property rights, the construction of a united society from groups of diverse peoples, the belief in progress, and the application of rational thought to public problems.

It has always struck me as strange that, for many European intellectuals, the United States is the society most associated with the edge between the present and the future. Because in many respects the United States is now closest to the zone between the present and the past. It is not accidental that the US landscape is one of the most modernist. All those straight lines, all those high-rise towers, all those disaffected modernist Europeans re-creating their intellectual systems. The United States became *the* country of modernism, the center for a whole range of movements in art, architecture, and social philosophy. Modernism was not place-less. Although a European invention, it found its most congenial home, its rationale, its most fertile breeding ground, and its most obvious embodiment in the United States. In many countries modernism and modernity only skimmed the surface of a deep pool. In the United States it was central, absolutely pivotal to the nation's view of itself.

To listen to contemporary debates in the United States is to hear the thunderous roar of giant tectonic plates as modernism and postmodernism collide. The concept of pluralism has re-placed the notion of the melting pot, obligations are now being discussed as much as rights, collective values are being counter-poised to rampant individualism, and even the national myth of the taming of the West has been reinterpreted as the defeat of the Indian Adam in the Eden of preurban, preindustrial, pre-Euro-pean America. Debates on ethnic identity, political correctness, and multiculturalism are at their most vigorous in the United States because of the centrality of modernist discourses at the heart of US political and intellectual life. In much of Europe, the modern was only one of many influences; in the United States, it was the defining moment and intellectual template of the society. The emergence of postmodernism is so contested in the United States because so much of the society's view of itself came from a modern perspective. The debates and intellectual struggle re-volving around modernism/postmodernism are ultimately about the changing meaning and significance of the United States.

Vernacular

The dictionary definition of this word refers to language: indigenous, spoken by the natives, not of foreign origin. Vernacular is local, related to a specific time and a particular place. In the modernist enterprise, the vernacular was seen as a temporary remnant of the past. In architecture, for example, the modern movement sought to replace the vernacular with the common syntax of straight lines, flat roofs, and smooth surfaces to be used around the world. Have design will travel. One element of the postmodern response is a resuscitation of vernacular forms and material; wood and brick as much as concrete and a referencing of the past as well as a celebration of the present.

The postmodern world is not a return to the vernacular. The world is too small, there are no *natives*. The past can only be recycled not relived. The postmodern world is one in which vernacular and universal, indigenous and foreign, global and local exist in a creative tension. The vernacular does not replace the universal—they exist side by side in a state of creative conflict, constant tension, and continual contact.

Wall Street

Wall Street is a street in Lower Manhattan in New York City whose name has become synonymous with financial wheeling and dealing; the measurement, moving, and making of money. It is not the biggest stock market in the world, that honor belongs to Japan. Wall Street in New York, the Marunouchi district in Tokyo, and the City in London are the three giant hubs of the global economy. They are the big links in the chain of capital that flows around the world. Their location around the world, their spacing in time ensures continuous trading.

Entrepreneurs used to make money by making things; steel, cars, videos, etc. Now they make money by moving money. Nothing much is made in reality (to use a modernist conceit) but selling stocks and shares, bonds and deeds can still lead to huge gains. The big profits are individually consumed, the big losses are shared by government and small investors.

Wall Street has been turned into celluloid. The movie of that name by Oliver Stone is a tale of a young man making money but losing his sense of right and wrong, a morality tale with the big investor/multimillionaire as the personification of evil.

A whole set of terms are now associated with Wall Street, including *junk bonds, asset stripping, yuppies, serious money, crisis,* and *crash.* Wall Street, like its equivalents in Japan and England, is the place of monetary dreams, financial scams, and fiscal nightmares; it is the site where money seems to have become a force out of control. Wall Street has become a sign of the times, a symbol of an economic system more responsive to individual greed than to social needs. As myth, Wall Street has become the setting where evil magicians cast their financial spells over a gullible, unsuspecting public. Wall Street has become a place of arcane rituals and diabolical plots, a stage for the evil Other.

Westerns

The basic subject matter of the western film genre is the fight between good and evil in the frontier zone between wilderness and civilization.

The early westerns celebrated the taming and ultimate defeat of the wilderness. One of the most successful silent epics was *The Covered Wagon* (1923), which told the story of a group of settlers moving west, overcoming buffalo stampedes and hostile Indians. A year later *The Iron Horse*, directed by John Ford, celebrated the coming of the railway and the "opening" up of the west. John Ford's subsequent career mirrors the development of the western. Through *Stagecoach* (1939) to *Rio Grande* (1950), the coming of white civilization was applauded, and the killing of Indians and the destruction of their culture was a regrettable though inevitable cost of the forward march of progress. In his last western, *Cheyenne Autumn* (1964), the heroes are the dispossessed, land-lost Indians. The coming of "civilization" is no longer seen as progress. This is the central focus of the postmodern westerns. The heroes of *Soldier Blue* (1970) or *Dances with Wolves* (1990) are the Indians. The villains are the imperialist whites. The taming of the "wilderness" and the coming of white power is a source of regret, not celebration. The notions of "progress" and "civilization" are problematic issues in the postmodern western. Just as they are in the postmodern world. Westerns tell us as much about contemporary concerns as they tell us about the past.

Yuppies

Yuppies were an invention of the 1980s; part fact, part fancy. They were part of a plethora of new words coined in the 1980s, including *bobos*, *dinkies*, *buppies*, *swells*, and (my favorite) *lombards*, which all referred to the emergence of a new middle class that was young, had high disposable incomes, few children, and no concept of deferred gratification. A yuppie was a young upwardly mobile person though the *u* also denoted *urban*. The other terms? *Bobos* were burned out but opulent; *dinkies* were double income, no kids; *buppies* were the yuppies' black equivalent, particularly important in the United States, while Britain had *swell*, a single women earning lots in London, a term summarizing the rise of the female executive and perhaps the beginnings of the end for the monopoly of the male domination of senior corporate positions. *Lombard* was lots of money but a right dickhead, a term of abuse whose real quality is only recognized if you know that one of the main streets in the City of London is Lombard Street. All these terms were both a recording of new trends and an advertising category. Yuppies were as much a function of ephemeral advertising campaigns as they were of solid economic processes.

As myths yuppies remain a powerful model, a peg for advertising campaigns, and dedicated followers of fashion. As fact yuppies were an emerging social group of the 1980s, with particular forms of employment and consumption. Their emergence was due to the rise of nonmanual and especially managerial and professional categories of employment. Yuppies are the higher-paid members of the technical management levels of the control centers of international corporations, the expanding financial services sector, producer services, and the media industry. They are particularly found in world cities such as New York and London, where these sectors are concentrated. The term *yuppie* is a loose one; it is suggestive of a new social group, not so much a class as a constellation of groups whose emergence has been noted but not fully identified.

Classes make themselves. Yuppies make themselves in their lifestyles, especially in attitudes to time and space. The filofax is the yuppie icon. It indicates the problem of time yet its successful management. It suggests a life full of work, commitments, movement, and meetings. It represents a full life. The problem with the unemployed, in contrast, is how to fill time. The cruel paradox of postmodern life is that those with more resources have less time, whereas those with most time have least resources. The attitude to time is matched by an assessment of space. Yuppies are inner-city dwellers. Their jobs are in the central areas. Not for them the trek to the suburbs made by their parents and dreamed of by their grandparents. A central location saves time in journey to work, entertainment, and contact with friends and influences. It is also symbolic of wider attitudes. The suburbs are, in essence, places for children, they indicate the willingness of people to lead their lives "for the children." Suburbs are places of sacrifice, sites for the reproduction of the nuclear family. The garden, the lower density, and the search for better schools are the essential ingredients of the suburban choice. Yuppie households, if they have children, are concerned as much with the wants of the adults as the perceived needs of the children.

As the 1980s turned into the 1990s, the term *yuppie* began to disappear as the economy faltered and the spend, spend, spend mentality of the 1980s fell out of favor as incomes declined and cultural norms shifted. Perhaps yuffies will replace yuppies as a cultural icon of the late 1990s. Yuffies are young urban failures. If the yuppies are the successful new middle class, yuffies are the declining middle class, the stranded working class, and the blocked underclass.

Zapper

A zapper is one of those little, black, plastic things that you use to change television channels without getting up from your seat. It is a piece of technological wizardry that we now take for granted. It is, however, more than just one more nifty piece of gadgetry.

One of the defining elements of postmodernism is a disbelief in metanarratives. The enemy is the defining narrative, the big story told by someone else. Television is a narrative. Stories are told, there are whole genres of taletelling, scripting, information transfer, transmission of moral values and political beliefs. In a very real sense, television is an ideological apparatus that structures our perception of the world. What the zapper does is to allow the listener/watcher a measure of control, a small space of creative editing. By being able to flick channels, the zapper is not simply a device for staying in your seat, it allows a measure of creative watching. No longer the passive audience sitting listening to someone else's edited television; the zapper allows the zapperee the opportunity to edit for themselves.

- Commercials come on. ZAP.
- A slow bit in the movie. ZAP.
- A boring guest on a talk show. ZAP.
- A distressing scene on the news. ZAP.

Television watchers, with the zapper in hand, can flick channels, change stories, edit their own narrative. Every zapperee their own editor, their own storyteller.

Creative watchers still have to use the raw material at hand. Choice depends on the number and range of channels. It is not simply the number of different channels that is important. Anyone who has seen the huge number of channels in many of the big cities in the United States soon realizes that fifty channels of garbage is still garbage, just lots of it. The more the variety of channels, the greater the opportunity for creating a more personal edit. There are still constraints. Only some stories are told, only certain beliefs are lauded. There is not a complete range of choice. But compared to the early years of television when one or two channels dominated the scene, today's multiplicity of channels and range of choices combined with the handy zapper allow more personal watching. There has been a decline in the mass audience. Only rarely does one program dominate the viewing so that it can become part of the gossip, chat, and discourse through which we keep in touch. Television has become less a social and more a personal experience.

The creative part only applies to those who hold the zapper.

There is no greater tyranny than watching television with other people and only one zapper, especially if someone else has the zapper. The capacity for freedom and the possibility for tyranny. Musing on that paradoxical ambiguity is as good a place as any to come to an end.

Or is it a beginning?

Publishing Acknowledgments

Suggested Readings

References

Publishing Acknowledgments

Although most of the material in this book was specifically written for it, some of the chapters have their origin and previous lives in other publications and forums.

Chapter 1 first saw the light of day as a postscript to the second edition of my book *An Introduction to Political Geography* (1993). It was a short summary of the major changes that had occurred since the first edition was published in 1982 and has been revised and amended for inclusion here.

Part of chapter 2 was first presented as a paper entitled "Old Nationalisms in the New Europe" to the International Geographical Union Commission on the World Political Map, in Prague, Czechoslovakia, August 26–30, 1991. This conference was the setting for the encounter that is described in the Introduction.

Part of Chapter 3 was first presented to a conference entitled "A New Urban and Regional Hierarchy," sponsored by the International Sociological Association and the University of California and held in Los Angeles in late April 1992. A few days after the conference ended, the city was engulfed in a social uprising. It also appears in my book *The Urban Order*.

Chapter 5 is part of a joint paper I wrote with Michelle Lowe under the same title that appeared in *Progress in Human Geography* in 1990. I owe the term *progressive human geography* to Michelle, who had been developing the idea some time before we met in 1987. I have (I hope) included only my contribution, although the whole enterprise was a joint one.

Chapter 6 first saw the light of day as a paper delivered to the Association of American Geographers' Annual Meeting held in San Diego, California, in April 1992.

Chapter 7 had two previous lives. One part of the paper was commissioned by the editors of the journal *Tijdschrift voor Economic en Sociale Geografie* as a response to a paper by Barney Warf. The other part of the paper was first published as "Three Problems Researching Place and Space" in the journal *Area* in 1989.

Chapter 8 has been through a number of transformations. It was first written as a banquet speech given to the 1992 Annual Meeting of the Middle States Division of the Association of American Geographers, held October 16, 1992, in Syracuse, New York. I was asked to make general comments on my experiences as a recent arrival interested in studying Central New York. It was subsequently published in 1993 in the *Newsletter* of the Association of American Geographers.

Suggested Readings

Barnes, Julian.

One of my favorite novelists. His range of work covers the literary to the personal to the political. Have a look at *Flaubert's Parrot* (1984), *Talking It Over* (1991), and *The Porcupine* (1992).

Harvey, David.
 1989, *The Condition of Postmodernity,* Oxford: Basil Blackwell.

A Marxist looks at the links between contemporary culture and contemporary capitalism. Some interesting remarks on space and time.

Hillman, James.
 1989, *A Blue Fire,* New York: Harper and Row.

One of our most consistent concerns is the subjective experience. And yet there are few new voices. Freud and Jung still dominate. One of the most explosive new voices is James Hillman. This book provides a wide sample of his work. At times it reads like Jung on crack or Freud on acid. Some of his sentences are either enigmatically brilliant or incomprehensible ramblings. Sometimes they are both. Hillman is one of those writers who has the capacity to change your angle of vision. His writings on a polytheistic psyche are in tune with the eclecticism of postmodernism.

Hughes, Robert.

1993, *Culture of Complaint*, New York: New York Public Library/Oxford Univ. Press.

Hughes is one of the most incisive, fearless, opinionated art critics. He has a wicked turn of phrase and a sensitive ear to public debates. Sometimes accurate, always entertaining.

Jameson, Frederick.

1991, *Postmodernism: The Cultural Logic of Late Capitalism*, Durham, N.C.: Duke Univ. Press.

A big name. A big book. Heavy in places.

Moore, Thomas.

1992, *Care of the Soul*, New York: HarperCollins.

Moore was the editor of Hillman's *Blue Fire*, and his writings gain insight from the same school of archetypal psychology. His beautifully crafted writing and humane learning combine to produce not so much a self-help book but a self-knowledge book that draws much from Greek myths and Renaissance learning. A suitably postmodern linkage of old and new.

National Geographic.

This journal, published every month since 1888, gives a sustained account of the Other. There are now enough back issues that some places and people have two or more entries over the years. Compare the entries and see how a modernist concern has been replaced by a postmodern pluralism.

Paglia. Camille.

1992, *Sex, Art and American Culture*, New York: Vintage.

A postfeminist iconoclast? A punchy, accessible style with a range of interests from Madonna to multiculturalism.

Said, Edward.

1992, *Culture and Imperialism*, New York: Knopf.

A literary critic who appears in the mass media, a Palestinian living in New York, a political dissident given airtime, an official radical with a tenured professorship at Columbia University. Edward Said embodies some of the paradoxes of the cultural critic. This book points to the importance of imperialism to the high culture of Europe; it is postcolonial literary criticism.

Films

Let me mention just three films that consider some of the themes raised in the A to Z. *The Crying Game* (1992) combines terrorism and sexual ambiguity. *Blade Runner* (1982) provides a picture of a possible future, complete with robots that look like humans and a Los Angeles that looks like Tokyo and New York combined under a black sky full of acid rain. The concern/rejection with authenticity, cultural xenophobia, and environmental doom rolled into one backdrop. Try to see the original version. A director's cut was released in 1992, but it lacks the narrative voice-over and the dramatic pacing of the original release. The studio got it right. *Thelma and Louise* (1991) is a road movie where there is violence, sex, and self-revelation. The feminist twist is that the protagonists are women. Watch it and wonder what a postfeminist road movie would look like. Or what about a postmodern, postfeminist, postcolonial, post-Fordist road movie?

References

Baldwin, James. 1967. Review of *The Arrangement. New York Review of Books*, Mar. 23, 17.

Bowman, Isaiah. 1922. *The New World: Problems in Political Geography.* London: Harrap.

Bruner, Jerome. 1986. "Two Modes of Thought." In *Actual Minds, Possible Worlds.* Cambridge, Mass.: Harvard Univ. Press.

Chomsky, Noam. 1973. *For Reasons of State.* London: Collins.

Davis, Mike. 1990. *City of Quartz.* London: Verso.

Dicken, Peter. 1986. *Global Shift.* London: Harper and Row.

Erlanger, S. 1993. "What Russia Wants." *New York Times*, Apr. 18, E1 and E5.

Fordham, Frieda. 1966. *An Introduction to Jung's Psychology.* Harmondsworth, England: Penguin.

Gardner, Howard. 1980. *Artful Scribbles.* New York: Basic.

Harvey, David. 1984. "On the History and Present Condition of Geography: An Historical Materialist Manifesto." *Professional Geographer* 36:1–11.

Kropotkin, Peter. 1885. "What Geography Ought to Be." *Nineteenth Century* 18:940–56.

Mackinder, Halford J. 1921. "Geography as a Pivotal Subject in Education." *Geographical Journal* 57:376–84.

McLuhan, Marshall. 1964. *Understanding Media: The Extensions of Man.* London: Routledge and Kegan Paul.

Miller, P. 1991. "Pittsburgh—Stronger than Steel." *National Geographic* (Dec.): 125–45.

Nairn, Tom. 1977. *The Break-up of Britain.* London: New Left.

Nichols, Tom, and Huw Benyon. 1977. *Living with Capitalism: Class Relations and the Modern Factory.* London: Routledge and Kegan Paul.

Rushdie, Salman (1996). "In Defense of the Novel, yet Again." *The New Yorker,* June 24 and July 1, 48–55.

Sacks, Oliver. 1987. *The Man Who Mistook His Wife for a Hat.* New York: Harper and Row.

Short, John. R. 1989. *The Humane City.* Oxford: Basil Blackwell.

———. 1989. "Yuppies, Yuffies and the New Urban Order." *Transactions of Institute of British Geographers,* n.s. 14:173–88.

———. 1996. *The Urban Order.* Oxford: Basil Blackwell.

Smith, David M. 1977. *Human Geography: A Welfare Approach.* London: Edward Arnold.

Storr, Anthony. 1988. *Solitude: A Return to the Self.* New York: Ballantine.

Warf, Barney. 1993. "Postmodernism and the Localities Debate." *Tijdschrift voor economische en sociale geografie,* 3: 158–68.